SELECTED POEMS

THOM GUNN

Selected Poems

Edited by Clive Wilmer

FABER & FABER

First published in 2017
by Faber & Faber Limited
Bloomsbury House
74–77 Great Russell Street
London WC1B 3DA

Typeset by Reality Premedia Services Pvt. Ltd.
Printed in Great Britain by Bell & Bain Ltd, Glasgow

A CIP record for this book
is available from the British Library

ISBN 978–0–571–32769–0

2 4 6 8 10 9 7 5 3

To Mike Kitay

Contents

Acknowledgements

I first read poems by Thom Gunn in 1962. He was generously represented in A. Alvarez's Penguin anthology *The New Poetry*, which had just been published. I had been encouraged by one of my schoolteachers, Peter Hilken, to read the book, and I remember him drawing my attention to Gunn's selection. Two years later, by luck and coincidence, I met Gunn himself in Cambridge; I was introduced to him by two of my teachers there – Helena Mennie Shire and Tony Tanner – quite independently of one another. This began a friendship of roughly forty years: an unusual friendship since – he living in California and I in Britain – it was mostly based on correspondence, and particularly on news and criticism of one another's writing. Despite the infrequency of our meetings, there are few people whose company I have enjoyed more. His poetry has meant more to me than that of any poet of my lifetime and I continue to feel a debt to him for the pleasure of reading him, and for the help and advice he gave me as a poet. He was always generous, considerate and, most valuable of all to a young writer, bluntly honest without ever being unkind.

In the preparation of this book I have had help from many people. I'd like to begin by thanking Ander Gunn for illuminating conversations and letters about his brother's life. My deepest gratitude is due to Thom's lifelong partner, Mike Kitay, and to the friends who share his house, Bob Bair and Billy Schuessler. They shared it with Thom, too, for several decades. I have stayed with them on a number of occasions, both in Thom's lifetime and while working on this book, and they have always been extremely kind and welcoming. They have also been generous with their time, talking over their memories with me – often, in

Mike's case, quite sensitive memories that are not easy to share. Mentioning them calls to mind another close friend of Thom's, August Kleinzahler, who lives two blocks away. Thom introduced me to him in 1986 and I have valued our many conversations in Britain and America ever since. I am also grateful to him for letting me read Gunn's letters to Douglas Chambers, of which he has copies.

Thanks are also due to Michael Nott for giving me transcripts of Gunn's letters to Karl Miller, which are held in Emory University Library, Atlanta, Georgia. I have used several libraries to do the research for this book, but the key one has been the Bancroft Library at Berkeley. I would like to thank the staff there for their helpfulness and efficiency, particularly Dean Smith, who has taken a personal interest in the work. I am also grateful to Sally Connolly for directing me to specific items in the Gunn collection there. My research would have been a great deal more laborious if it had not been for Gunn's bibliographers. Jack W. C. Hagstrom, the author with George Bixby of *Thom Gunn: A Bibliography* (London: Bertram Rota Publishing, 1979), first visited me in the 1970s and was very kind. He and Joshua S. Odell have now produced a new edition of that bibliography, revised, and expanded by the addition of a second volume (New Castle, DE: Oak Knoll Press, 2013). I would like to express my thanks, both personally and professionally, to both Jack and Joshua.

This book was commissioned for Faber & Faber by Paul Keegan, whose idea it was. I'd like to thank him for his generosity and friendliness, for inviting me to read the Gunn correspondence in the Faber & Faber archive, and for the idea of a selection significantly amplified by quotations from the poet's essays, letters, readings and conversations. The book has changed a little under my new editor, Matthew Hollis, but I have tried to keep Paul's original conception in mind. I could name a great many friends and acquaintances with whom I have talked about Gunn to my great profit over the years, but I will confine myself to three. They are all poets themselves and were all admired by Gunn: Dick Davis, Michael Vince and Robert Wells. Gunn's poetry has been meat and drink to the four of us for more than fifty years and I couldn't have done without them.

CW

Abbreviations and References

For Thom Gunn's name I use the initial G. For his books I have used the following abbreviations:

Collected Poems	CP
Fighting Terms	FT
The Sense of Movement	SM
My Sad Captains	MSC
Jack Straw's Castle	JSC
The Passages of Joy	PJ
The Man with Night Sweats	MNS
Boss Cupid	BC
The Occasions of Poetry	OP
Shelf Life	SL

The notes often refer to interviews with Gunn. These are abbreviated as follows:

WS W. I. Scobie in *London Magazine* (December 1977)

JH John Haffenden, *Viewpoints: Poets in Conversation* (London: Faber & Faber, 1981)

CH Christopher Hennessy, 'An Interview with Thom Gunn', *Outside the Lines: Talking With Contemporary Gay Poets* (Ann Arbor: University of Michigan, 2005)

PR Clive Wilmer in *The Paris Review* 35 (135) (Summer 1995)

JC *Thom Gunn in Conversation with James Campbell* (London: Between the Lines, 2000)

Gunn's private papers – notebooks, diaries, letters, etc.

– are kept at the Bancroft Library, University of California (Berkeley), abbreviated as 'Bancroft'. They include the letters of John Holmstrom (JH/Bancroft) and those of Belle Randall (BR/Bancroft). Gunn's correspondence with his publishers, Faber & Faber (F&F), are held in the Faber offices in London. Letters to Tony Tanner (TT) are in the library of King's College, Cambridge, those to Karl Miller (KM) at Emory University, Atlanta, Georgia. Those written to, and held by, the present editor are referred to by the initials CW.

Bible references are to the Authorised (King James) Version. Shakespeare references are to *The Complete Works*, ed. Stanley Wells and Gary Taylor (Oxford: Clarendon Press, 1986).

Introduction

From 1956 to 1966, the *Observer* had a poetry editor, the critic
A. Alvarez. Even in those days it was not to be expected that
newspapers would publish poetry, but there was a renewed
interest in the art and Alvarez's enthusiasms were playing
a part in it. He spoke up for a poetry that lived 'on the edge'
and championed young authors impatient with what he called
'gentility', then (as he saw it) the prevailing vice of middle-class
English culture. Pretty well every week the *Observer* published a
poem, often several poems, and the poets given most prominence
were Ted Hughes, Sylvia Plath and Thom Gunn, all then in their
late twenties and early thirties. In 1962 Alvarez published an
anthology of the poets he admired: *The New Poetry*. It began
with two Americans, Robert Lowell and John Berryman, and
represented Gunn and Hughes substantially. (A revised edition
included Plath and Anne Sexton.) That same year, 1962, also
saw the publication of the *Selected Poems* of Thom Gunn and
Ted Hughes, an attempt by their publisher, Faber & Faber, to
showcase the two young men who were increasingly seen as the
major figures in an expanding market. This book became an A
level set text and, partly as a result, was reprinted six times over
the next eleven years. It sold 81,500 copies: a spectacular success
for a book of poetry.

Lowell, Berryman, Plath and Sexton came to be known, rightly
or wrongly, as Confessional poets, all of them dealing with
extreme forms of personal experience – breakdown, depression,
suicide and so on. Alvarez himself preferred to speak of 'extremist'
poetry, and in that category he was also able to include Ted
Hughes, who was noticed for the violence in his work. But what
about Gunn? He undoubtedly had a preoccupation with what

Browning called 'the dangerous edge of things', but he seemed to be a different kind of poet. Some readers of the Gunn/Hughes selection found him difficult, intellectual, too strictly formal, even cold. Gunn was gay at a time when gay people tended not to be open about themselves. He had also lived in the United States for some years and his language had begun to hover between British and American usage. Yet, despite his evident obsessions with leather boys, biker gangs, rock 'n' roll and the nightlife of sprawling American cities, he did not expose an inner self. People used to talk in the 1960s – perhaps they still do – about true poets 'finding their own voices'. Gunn appeared not to have a distinctive voice. Indeed, he appeared to have no wish to find one. What he aspired to achieve in poetry was something he found in Elizabethan song – for instance in a song he was fond of quoting, Thomas Campion's 'Now winter nights enlarge':

> This time doth well dispense
>   With lovers' long discourse.
> Much speech hath some defence
>   Though beauty no remorse.
> All doe not all things well:
>   Some measures comely tread,
> Some knotted Ridles tell,
>   Some Poems smoothly read.
> The Summer hath his joyes,
>   And Winter his delights;
> Though Love and all his pleasures are but toyes,
>   They shorten tedious nights.

There is in this a certain anonymity of tone, which Gunn sought to emulate. He began by doing so in poems constructed with a comparable musical structure. He later became interested in the open forms of avant-garde American writing, but even in those poems, with their free verse and colloquial turns of phrase, there remains an impersonal touch. Take, for example, this passage from his 'Sweet Things', in which a street encounter leads to a sexual proposition:

> Boldly 'How about now?' I say
> knowing the answer. My boy
> I could eat you whole. In the long pause
> I gaze at him up and down and
> from his blue sneakers back to the redawning
> one-sided smile. We know our charm.
> We know delay makes pleasure great.
> In our eyes, on our tongues,
> we savour the approaching delight
> of things we know yet are fresh always.
> Sweet things. Sweet things.

In the last six lines of this passage, Gunn veers away from the personal, the local, the modern, even the specifically gay, and reaches for the general – for a kind of truism, but truism grounded in feeling and experience (as the context reminds us). At this point in the poem, the speaker's first-person 'I' is replaced by 'we' and the rhythm briefly shifts to something like the iambic tetrameter:

> We know our charm.
> We know delay makes pleasure great.

It is not only in Campion or his contemporary John Dowland that we find this but sometimes in Shakespeare and Jonson, to say nothing of Sappho and Catullus. At the same time, no one could accuse the poem of not being modern or of naively aspiring to the universal.

This taste in Gunn for truism and the impersonal tone went with an attitude to his subject matter that was unfashionable. He was not interested in self-expression. He didn't write to give a voice to interior anguish. He had a good deal, in fact, to feel anguished about, but, as he suggests in another rather casual free-verse poem, 'Expression', he didn't want to give dramatic expression to it. The students in his creative writing class write, he tells us,

> of breakdown, mental institution,
> and suicide attempt, of which the experience
> does not always seem first-hand.
> It is very poetic poetry.

Impatient with this, he turns for relief to an 'early Italian' Madonna and Child in the nearby art gallery:

> The sight quenches, like water
> after too much birthday cake.
> Solidly there, mother and child
> stare outward, two pairs of matching eyes
> void of expression.

The absence of expression refreshes because it turns the matter of poetry outward – towards the world. In an essay on William Carlos Williams, Gunn praises that master for being more interested in the world than in himself.

Some of Gunn's poetry, like some of Williams's, seeks simply to register real things, because the interest of things is independent of human emotion. At the same time, Gunn is conscious that putting things into words is also, from the start, an attempt to make sense of them. This view of language was emphatically endorsed for Gunn in the 1950s by his teacher, the Californian poet Yvor Winters, who recommended the poems of Ben Jonson. Jonson became something of a touchstone for Gunn. Jonson prefaced his book of epigrams, *The Underwood* (1640), with this couplet:

> Pray thee, take care, that tak'st my booke in hand,
> To reade it well: that is, to understand.

Gunn comments on this in the introduction to his selection of Jonson's poems in the Penguin Poet to Poet series (1974): 'The process of understanding', he wrote, amounts to something 'more than the business of comprehending the text . . . Understanding means taking [the poems] to heart, means – ultimately – *acting* on them' (OP, p. 110).

It was Gunn's misfortune that this highly moralistic view of poetry and its purposes was not what most people wanted to hear in the later twentieth century. While 'extremist' preoccupations seemed to prevail in his work he remained fashionable, but by the late 1960s he had moved on to a more humanistic mode of writing, which first communicated itself in his 1967 volume *Touch*. The high point of his humanistic poetry was attained – paradoxically, it might seem – in a volume of poems about drug-inspired visions and experiences: *Moly*, published in 1971. In these volumes, Gunn came across as a fully adopted Californian and also as a much happier man than he had at first seemed. The result – in Britain, at any rate – was a drastically reduced readership at precisely that point in his life when (as it will probably now seem) he was writing at his best. The strange thing was that, if private conversation is to be relied on, he cared very little about fame. I once mentioned to him my disquiet as to how unjustly he was estimated. He was silent for a minute and then said, 'I think I'm famous enough.' I have come to think that the loss of his youthful celebrity gave him a kind of freedom to experiment.

Freedom, at any rate, was of the essence. In a memoir of his time as an undergraduate, published in 1977, he tells this story:

> . . . one day, hitch-hiking along a long narrow dusty road in France, I experienced a revelation of physical and spiritual freedom that I still refer to in my thoughts as the Revelation. It was like the elimination of some enormous but undefined problem that had been across my way and prevented me from moving forward. But now I suddenly found I had the energy for almost anything. And wherever I was . . . I pushed myself through an apprenticeship in poetry. I was greatly influenced by Auden still . . . And Donne gave me the licence to be obscure and to find material in the contradictions of one's own emotions.
>
> (OP, p. 159)

The key words in this passage are 'freedom' and 'energy'. Gunn called his second book *The Sense of Movement*, conscious that 'sense' can mean both 'meaning' and 'sensation'. The ambiguity sums up his poetry. For him, the starting point was the feeling of freedom and the energy it enabled. He would talk of the sensation of feeling full of energy. It was almost like a mystical experience: the consciousness of simply being alive. It caused him to want to turn physical into verbal energy. What the energy permitted in the poems was – to quote again – 'the contradictions of one's own emotions': it allowed him to bring together the animal and the intellectual, openness and closure, morality and hedonism; to believe in 'the hippie values' of love, trust and peace alongside a taste for promiscuous, sadomasochistic sex; to draw equally on Elizabethan song and the poetry of the American avant-garde.

Thom Gunn was born in Gravesend, Kent, on the southern bank of the Thames Estuary. The date was 29 August 1929. His name was registered as William Guinneach Gunn, Guinneach being an old family name on his father's side, but for most of his childhood he was known as 'Tom'. His parents were both of Scottish origin. They were journalists and had met while working for a local newspaper. His father, Herbert Gunn, was to become a successful national editor, notably of the tabloid *Daily Sketch*. Gunn's relationship with him was to prove difficult; something of his ambivalence is expressed in the monologue 'From an Asian Tent': 'each year [I] look more like the man I least / Choose to resemble, bully, drunk, and beast' (p. 47). He was by contrast extremely close to his mother. Charlotte Gunn (née Thomson) was the source of Gunn's enthusiasm for literature; she was also (as he was) politically rather left-wing and inclined to be unconventional. Gunn cherished her memory throughout his life – indeed, two of the key poems in his final collection are directly concerned with her (see pp. 183–85). He once remarked that 'from her I absorbed the idea of books as a part of life, not merely a commentary on it' (WS, p. 7). In his conversation he frequently referred to the books he had read with passion as a child and many of these he would reread as an adult from time to time. The ones I particularly remember him mentioning are Beatrix Potter's *The Tale of Samuel Whiskers*, George MacDonald's *At the Back of the North Wind*, Lewis Carroll's Alice books, Nathaniel Hawthorne's *Tanglewood Tales*, Robert Louis Stevenson's *A Child's Garden of Verses* and *Kidnapped*, and, above all, the novels of E. Nesbit. Most of these books had some influence on poems included in this selection. It is my private suspicion that he associated Nesbit – 'that sensible woman', he used to call her – with his mother, who shared Nesbit's utopian politics and her sense of the practical value of literature.

In 1938 the Gunns moved to Hampstead in north London. Hampstead is one of the city's wealthiest districts and a famously cultured one, so the move no doubt reflected Bert Gunn's rising income and status. By this time there was a younger brother, Alexander, who came to be known as Ander. The common land of Hampstead Heath became the boys' playground. Both were later to attend University College School, which was round the corner from their home. UCS was an elite grammar school and Gunn did well there, though he was evacuated to Bedales in Hampshire during the war.

Gunn always described his early childhood as 'happy', which it does seem by and large to have been, but in 1940 his parents, always incompatible, divorced. Both of them soon remarried, the boys staying with their mother and her new husband. Before long, however, her second marriage failed and, on 29 December 1944, she committed suicide. Her body was discovered by her sons, an experience later reflected on in 'The Gas-poker' (p. 184). There is an extraordinary account of their discovery of the body in Gunn's diary for that day. I have included it in the notes to this edition (pp. 270–72).

It was accepted that Thom and his father could not get on, so while Ander went to live with Bert Gunn's new family, Thom lodged with a friend of his mother's in Hampstead. Weekends and holidays he spent with two of his mother's six sisters, unmarried aunts who ran what had been his grandfather's farm at Snodland in rural Kent. Gunn retained feelings of gratitude and affection towards these women throughout his life. It is an important fact about Gunn that – lover of great cities though he was – he had roots and affections in the countryside.

In his late teens Gunn retreated into himself, literature becoming both a passion and a means of escape. A more confident identity began to emerge when, in 1950, after two years of national service in the army and six months working in Paris, he went up to Trinity College, Cambridge, to read English. The previous year he had changed his name by deed poll to Thomson William Gunn, Thomson being his mother's maiden name. It is important to note that this new self-assurance involved the replacement of a name from his father's family with his mother's maiden name. He had always been known as Tom, but in what he later recognised as 'an attempt to become a new person', he now began to use the spelling Thom (JC, p. 21). The new combination, Thom Gunn, with its two strong syllables and its evocation of 'tomcat' and 'tommy gun', suggests a highly masculine self-image that was probably at this stage at odds with much in his overt behaviour. He was introspective, highly sensitive and beginning to be aware of his homosexuality. Ander Gunn remembers their father in angry mood referring to his elder son as a 'pansy'.

Cambridge nourished Thom's imagination. He began publishing poetry of striking maturity in student magazines and befriended other writers. His passion for Elizabethan poetry was nurtured by a congenial supervisor, the medievalist Helena Mennie Shire, to whom he remained close in later life. He also attended the lectures of the celebrated F. R. Leavis, whose insistence on the importance to poetry of 'realisation' helped to shape Gunn's firm and energetic style. It also reinforced his mother's lessons about the relevance of literature to life. Under such influences he could think of himself as a modern follower of Donne and Shakespeare, who, as he said, 'spoke living language to me . . . one I tried to turn to my own uses' (OP, p. 173). His confidence in the value of his work was enhanced by the critical interest of student friends, most notably the future critic and editor Karl Miller, and the star actor among a group of theatrical friends, Anthony White.

Gunn's sense of Shakespeare's relevance was enhanced by the vitality at this time of student theatre at Cambridge. Peter Hall and John Barton, both undergraduate contemporaries of Gunn's, were active in it. Their emerging talent and the support of a senior academic, George Rylands, made for high-quality acting and production. Tony White was beguiling and charismatic, with a beautiful voice and a powerful stage presence. He played several great classical roles, mostly in Shakespeare, 'as romantic-existentialist characters'. Gunn was strongly attracted to him, but White was heterosexual, and his elusiveness, as Gunn experienced it, played its part in the development of his poetry. The elusiveness was not only due to his different orientation. It was part of the existential loneliness that, despite the depth of his dramatic talent, kept him away from what Gunn calls 'the life of applause' (OP, p. 168). In the loneliness occasioned by the loss of his mother, Gunn must have perceived White as in some sense an alter ego. They remained close friends until White's premature and accidental death at the age of forty-five. The sequence 'Talbot Road' (pp. 144–50) is a study of his charisma.

As this story suggests, it was in Cambridge that Gunn was able to acknowledge his homosexuality, if only to himself and to close friends. In the same dramatic circles where Gunn met White, he was soon attracted to another handsome young man, an American student named Mike Kitay. They met on 7 December 1952 and quickly fell in love. Both of them were still quite innocent. Before their meeting, Kitay had not been conscious of being gay and Gunn was still without serious experience. The American's attractions brought in their wake a tenderness and intimacy new to Gunn, even in time a certain domesticity. Kitay was to become Gunn's lifelong companion and the addressee of many of his poems (e.g. 'Tamer and Hawk', p. 9; and 'The Hug', p. 157). Gunn describes him as 'the leading influence on my life' and writes of their relationship as long-lasting, deep and complex: 'his was, from the start, the example of the searching worrying improvising intelligence playing upon the emotions which in turn reflect back on the intelligence. It was an example at times as rawly passionate as only Henry James can dare to be' (OP, p. 175). They must have looked like complementary opposites: Kitay emotionally open, affectionate, a little needy; Gunn inclined to solitude, inwardly vulnerable, armoured against such feelings as might wound him. My metaphors in that last clause are Gunn's, of course. See, for instance, the first poem in this selection, 'The Wound', the first poem in all Gunn's own selections and collections of his work (p. 5). Gunn remained in many ways a solitary person. In middle life, though he remained attached to Kitay and dedicated to him as a partner, he opted for a life of sexual promiscuity, and it could be said that in this, paradoxically, his solitude reasserted itself. Certainly in the first three books the 'romantic existentialist' (to borrow that description of White) is overwhelmingly in evidence.

By the time he graduated in 1953, Gunn's first book of poems, *Fighting Terms* (1954), had been accepted for publication by the small Fantasy Press. The poems explored themes of heroism and masculinity and were dominated by the image of the soldier. Most of them were apprentice work, though a handful – 'The Wound' is perhaps the most famous of them – remain among his most memorable. That poem represents the soldier in his full complexity: he is Achilles sulking or angry, he is the disengaged conscript that Gunn had actually been, he is a young man seized by violent emotion who, in his dreams, fights 'on both sides'.

In the same year as the appearance of *Fighting Terms*, Gunn was awarded a Graduate Fellowship at Stanford University, California. His aim in applying had been to follow Kitay to the United States, but he had the good fortune, at Stanford, to study under Yvor Winters: poet, critic and charismatic teacher. Under Winters, for a time, Gunn found the discipline he needed for his poetry. That discipline was perhaps a defence against emotional damage, but like the influence (far less personal) of Leavis, it also taught him that poetry could be true to the demands of waking life. Winters is widely thought to have been a chilly, cerebral autocrat. This is quite wrong. Winters's poems are distinguished, at their best, by formal elegance, moral alertness and what Gunn calls, in his introduction to Winters's *Selected Poems* (New York: Library of America, 2003), 'the sensory sharpness of Imagism'. He loved great poetry as passionately as it is possible to love it, as Gunn often testified, but his criteria for great poetry had severely narrowed with time. Writing to Karl Miller not long after starting work at Stanford, Gunn says this:

I'm working under Yvor Winters, who has something of the same position in America as Leavis does in England. The same stubbornness, rudeness, feeling of persecution once justified but no longer justified. His critical position is just about that of Dr Johnson if Dr J were alive today – rather too much common sense, and an acute dislike of anything 'romantic', which term includes Lawrence, Yeats, & Eliot. So, as you see, he's a good deal more limited than Leavis, tho I can't help admiring him, and like him personally a good deal.

(KM, 26 November 1954)

Winters, who had reacted against an early attraction to Modernism, insisted on formal precision and rational order in poetry. He nonetheless urged Gunn to read the American Modernists Wallace Stevens and William Carlos Williams, who were still little known in Britain. Gunn's own reputation as an anti-Modernist was further enhanced when he was included by Robert Conquest in *New Lines* (1956), the anthology of the so-called Movement: nine poets, including Philip Larkin and Donald Davie, whose work combined strict traditional form with irony, wit and critical perspectives on modern life. But though Gunn was pleased at being anthologised, he never identified with the Movement poets. He was less conservative than they were, more individualistic, more rebellious and not uninterested in Modernism.

Gunn's next book, *The Sense of Movement* (1957), is strongly indebted to Winters and includes a notable tribute to him – 'To Yvor Winters, 1955'(pp. 25–26) – which is very much in the master's manner. The debt is partly to be found in the crisply formal versification that Gunn had now mastered, and partly in the severe stoicism, which now added depth to his earlier heroics. *The Sense of Movement* is distinguished by Metaphysical wit and a strict but elegant formality. Gunn's love of the big modern city, influenced by Baudelaire and enhanced by his new experience of urban America, is apparent in many of them. There is a poem about Elvis Presley turning 'revolt into a style' (p. 21), and in 'On the Move' (pp. 15–16) Gunn captures the mood of the time with his image of Californian bikers forging their own direction through an uncertain world: like Marlon Brando in his film *The Wild One* translated into the language of existentialism. Pictures of Brando, James Dean and Elvis Presley joined Donne and Baudelaire on the wall of Gunn's study.

Gunn had also been reading the work of Jean-Paul Sartre, both the novels and an important essay, *L'Existentialisme est un humanisme* (1946; translated into English by Philip Mairet as *Existentialism and Humanism*, 1948). In such poems as 'On the Move', Sartre's philosophy combined improbably with the ideas of Yvor Winters and with W. B. Yeats, whose poetry, not much admired by Winters, Gunn had recently discovered. As Gunn tells us, both Winters and Sartre talked a great deal about will. Gunn later mocked himself by pointing out that they meant quite different things by it, but that he had fused their ideas together with what he called a Yeatsian wilfulness that would not have been attractive to either of them.

Meanwhile, the stoicism and the admiration of masculine strength and will served to express, and simultaneously to mask, his fascination with the gay subculture of San Francisco. He claimed to have been unconscious of the fact that, in

Shakespeare's English, 'will' is a common colloquialism for the penis, one which survives in the childhood euphemism 'willy'. It is difficult to believe that, when he wrote about leather-clad bikers 'astride the created will' in 'On the Move' and how 'their hum / Bulges to thunder held by calf and thigh', he was not talking about masculine sexuality, but at the time even his critics somehow failed to notice. The poems had, as it were, a double life. Outwardly they displayed the stern discipline admired by Winters; inwardly they explored desires that in both Britain and America fell outside the law. Much the same applied to Gunn's personal life, in which he had to keep his desires hidden, like the young man in 'The Allegory of the Wolf Boy' (p. 22). At Stanford he wore a suit and tie. When night fell, he changed into the new gay 'uniform': white T-shirt, leather jacket, jeans and motorcycling boots. There came to be something of the dandy about him. Before long, he had a panther tattooed the length of one arm, a broad strap of black leather as a watch strap and a bunch of keys hanging from his cowboy belt.

In 1958 Gunn became an instructor at the University of California, Berkeley, where he was to teach off and on until 1999. He and Kitay now shared a San Francisco apartment. The year 1961 saw the publication of *My Sad Captains*, a book divided into halves, the first developing and complicating the heroic manner of *The Sense of Movement*, the second experimenting with the 'unpatterned rhythms' of syllabic verse (OP, p. 179): verse, that is to say, in which the syllables are counted but not the accents or feet. The freer rhythms involved in syllabics allowed Gunn to register observations of a less obviously momentous kind. The poems are no less profound, however. 'Considering the Snail' (p. 41), which asks half humorously, 'What is a snail's fury?', provides some sort of an answer to the large questions posed in 'On the Move'. It is also arguably a finer poem. Under the influence of William Carlos Williams and Marianne Moore,

Gunn was learning to be more of a humanist and opening himself up to Modernist experiment. As he always insisted, his work in syllabics was a stage on the road to free verse, which he had earlier found difficult to write. This is undoubtedly true, but I think it does not do justice to his achievements in syllabics to see the work as simply a staging post. As in Marianne Moore's poetry, most of which is written in syllabics too, the poems seem to uncover the poetry latent in prose, often unsensationally prosaic prose. At any rate, the title poem of his next full collection, *Touch* (1967), reveals a new Gunn able to write without the overt constraints of either iambic metre or syllabics. This is true free verse and 'Touch' (pp. 56–57) is one of Gunn's finest achievements. In it, for the first time, he is able to write a poetry of process, in which he appears to be thinking aloud, reflecting on his circumstances as they change and develop. Such a poetry is in striking contrast to the monumental closure of his metrical verse. From the mid-1960s on, he made it his business to master both methods.

Why would a poet who moved so confidently in the standard English metres, and insisted, moreover, on the need for discipline, feel this need to work in a new and looser medium? The answer must lie in part in the poetry Gunn had discovered in America: the poetry of Whitman, Pound and Williams, as well as that of Robert Creeley, Allen Ginsberg and Gary Snyder. There was also a theoretical interest inspired by an essay of D. H. Lawrence's. In the Preface to his *New Poems* (1920), Lawrence talks of free verse as pre-eminently the medium of present-tense meditation, of perception in the process of taking form. Most poetry, he says, deals with ends and beginnings, with past and future:

It is in the realm of all that is perfect. It is of the nature of all that is complete and consummate. This completeness, this consummateness, the finality and the perfection are conveyed in exquisite form . . . But there is another kind of poetry: the poetry of that which is at hand: the immediate present. In the immediate present there is no perfection, no consummation, nothing finished.

(D. H. Lawrence, 'Introduction to New Poems', *Selected Literary Criticism*, ed. Anthony Beal, London: Heinemann, 1956, pp. 84–89)

The incompleteness Lawrence talks about had always been part of Gunn's subject matter, inseparable from his preoccupation with energy. As he says in 'On the Move', 'One is always nearer by not keeping still', and 'One moves . . . always toward, toward'. The excitement of Gunn's earlier poetry had lain in the tension between form and content, yet it is not surprising that he should also have come to admire a poetry which possessed the very qualities that moved him in real life.

In the 1980s and 1990s, Gunn was to talk about his poetry in terms of 'openness' and 'closure', terms derived largely from post-modern theory but associated in his thinking with the ideas and practice of the fiercely experimental poet Robert Duncan, who became a friend of Gunn's in the 1970s. Gunn was very much inspired, not always to good effect, by Duncan's notion of the poem as a process, as a construct that was essentially incomplete. But as his elegy for Duncan, written in strictly metrical form, suggests, there remained in his mind occasions to which a poetry of closure, Lawrence's poetry of the past, was more appropriate than a poetry of openness such as Duncan's. (See 'Duncan', pp. 181–82, and the note for it on pp. 268–69.) In the late 1960s and early 1970s, many of Gunn's contemporaries on both sides of the Atlantic abandoned metre in favour of free verse. Gunn by contrast continued to regard free verse and orthodox metre as viable alternatives. Free verse became a new string to his bow, but metre continued to make some things possible that were not possible without it. It is noteworthy that at two key periods of his subsequent life – in the late 1960s, when he was experimenting with psychedelic drugs, and in the late 1980s, when numbers of his friends began dying of AIDS – he produced bodies of work in iambic metre that stand among his finest achievements.

The alternation between old and new manners, however, was not always productive. He was never happy with *Touch*, which he thought dull, over-moralistic and uncertain in direction. Much of it was, paradoxically, the outcome of a very productive year, 1964–65, spent in London. The carnival atmosphere of 'swinging London' and the sound of joyful rebellion made by the Beatles appealed to Gunn's temperament. He had written a book of verse captions for photographs by his brother, Ander (*Positives*, 1965; see p. 223), and completed a long sequence, 'Misanthropos' (pp. 58–79), about the lone survivor of a nuclear war. It was in *Positives* that he first achieved the transition from syllabics to free verse, and it was there, too, that he began to work out a more humanistic attitude to life. The early work had been largely heroic in tone. In the first half of *My Sad Captains*, very much under the influence of Albert Camus, who had replaced Sartre in his enthusiasms, Gunn began wondering what heroic action would be in 'a valueless world' (to quote from 'On the Move'). As in Camus's novel *The Plague* (1947), moral action is an arbitrary choice; it brings no advantage with it, except the affirmation of our humanity. Two poems about Nazi Germany exemplified this outlook: 'Innocence' (pp. 33–34) evokes the career of a young SS officer whose amoral upbringing has resulted in moral numbness, while Claus von Stauffenberg, in the poem of that name, motivated by love of honour 'In a cold time where honour cannot grow', refuses to accept that 'An unsanctioned present must be primitive' (p. 38). In a quieter and more circumstantial way, the *Positives* captions look affectionately at what it is to be human. They do so in a manner that Gunn had learned in part from the poems of Williams, on whom at the time he was writing a groundbreaking essay (OP, pp. 21–35). 'Misanthropos', which he included in *Touch*, brings these different elements together. It even includes a poem, 'Epitaph for Anton Schmidt', which deliberately calls to mind the German poems from *My Sad Captains*. But there are also syllabic poems, which show Gunn as a poet able to respond imaginatively to fortuitous circumstance. 'Misanthropos' is not an unqualified success. The first two-thirds of the poem is as good as anything Gunn wrote and seems to anticipate a work of real authority, but the last section, in which the persona rediscovers his humanity, suffers from crude didacticism and plods rather heavily along.

The moral of 'Misanthropos' is that we rediscover our humanity through *touch*: not through willing ourselves to virtue but by opening up to others. This is the theme of the title poem, 'Touch', which is probably the finest of Gunn's love poems. Getting into bed with his sleeping lover, the speaker rediscovers the warmth of their shared lives. 'You are already / asleep', he begins, and then ends with an echo of that beginning:

> What I, now loosened,
> sink into is an old
> big place, it is
> there already, for
> you are already
> there . . .
> . . . the place is
> not found but seeps
> from our touch in
> continuous creation, dark
> enclosing cocoon round

ourselves alone, dark
wide realm where we
walk with everyone.

With its short lines and stark enjambments it is very much
a poem of process; it calls to mind the style of Robert Creeley,
though the content is reminiscent of John Donne. What the
process seems to reveal is the recovery of a warmth the speaker
and his partner had been losing. This reflects something of Gunn's
life in the late 1960s. Growing away from armoured solitude
seems to have involved becoming more openly promiscuous, a
development that was eventually to loosen his relationship with
Mike Kitay. In 1972 Gunn bought a house on Cole Street in
Haight-Ashbury, the 'hippie' district of San Francisco. He and
Kitay expanded their relationship to include other men, their
own relationship ceasing to be sexual, and the house became,
in effect, a gay commune – or as Gunn, ever one to *épater les
bourgeois*, liked to say: 'a queer household' (PR, p. 150). The
changes in social mores associated with the 1960s were spreading
across the world and San Francisco was in the vanguard. Young
people were 'dropping out' and 'turning on', and Gunn, Kitay
and their friends identified with them. They attended the free
rock concerts in Golden Gate Park and experimented with the
mind-expanding drug LSD. These experiences and a personal
quest to rediscover human innocence resulted in the achievement
of which Gunn was most proud: *Moly* (1971) can be read as a
single work on the themes of metamorphosis, evolving identity,
and the physical world as paradise. The title refers to a magical
herb that features in Homer's *Odyssey*. In Gunn's book, it stands
for the consciousness-changing drugs, such as LSD, with which
he was experimenting.

The *Moly* poems represent (to borrow from a title of William
Empson's) a version of pastoral. They recall that element in the

Elizabethan poetry Gunn so loved. They also revive the early vision of America as the new paradise, uninfected by the sins of the Old World. In one of the poems not included here ('To Natty Bumppo'), Gunn says of a field:

> Open on all sides, it is held in common,
> The first field of a glistening continent
> Each found by trusting Eden in the human

But though he insists on the utopian element implicit in the words 'open', 'trusting' and 'in common', he is also aware of the conflicts and complexes that occupy the human interior. The dope-peddler who, in 'Street Song' (pp. 94–95), brings the possibility of visionary experience, proposes his inward journey in these terms:

> Call it heaven, call it hell,
> Join me and see the world I sell.
>
> Join me, and I will take you there,
> Your head will cut out from your hair
> Into whichever self you choose.

This is surely alarming. It is not only that we might not care to risk hell, but that the *choice* of selves is not, to most of us, an obvious benefit either. Gunn's exploration of his own identity, moreover, is hardly confined to the terms of love and peace. The opening poem of the collection, 'Rites of Passage' (p. 85), evokes an Ovidian metamorphosis that is plainly to be understood in terms of the Oedipus complex: a fierce conflict between the hated father and the desired mother, the latter long dead and buried but still insistently present to the poet as his Muse. In his notebooks and conversation Gunn would insist on the femininity of the Muse, even in the imagination of a gay man. This is the subject of a fine earlier poem, 'The Goddess' (p. 55), and is firmly stated here: 'I stamp upon the earth / A message to my mother.'

The utopian pastoral of the *Moly* poems found its antithesis in the much less successful volume that succeeded it, *Jack Straw's Castle* (1976). The poems that open the collection, all in traditional metre, to some extent continue and develop the world of *Moly*; but the title poem and a group of free verse poems related to it disclose the darker consequences of the drug culture. The castle of the title is partly the human body and partly the usual setting for 'Gothick' nightmare. It is presided over by the notorious 'hippie' psychopath Charles Manson, who had driven the members of the so-called 'Manson family' to commit nine murders at their commune in the Californian desert. The book concludes on a gentler note, however, with a number of autobiographical poems, mostly about Gunn's former life in England. *Jack Straw's Castle* is an uneven collection, but it marks a significant change in Gunn's work: it was in the title poem, for instance, that Gunn 'came out' as a gay poet, having masked his orientation in earlier books. From now on, Gunn had at his disposal a substantial range of new subject matter.

For most of the 1960s, Gunn had been an Associate Professor at Berkeley. He was by all accounts an effective and charismatic teacher of English literature and creative writing, as poets such as Jim Powell, Belle Randall and Joshua Weiner, all taught by him, have testified. Temperamentally, teaching suited him. He liked the daytime discipline: he read and wrote on the bus journeys across the Bay Bridge to work. Teaching, moreover, kept him in touch with the young, as with the need for poetry to communicate. In the early 1970s, however, he decided to go part-time in order to give himself more freedom to write. He was eventually to return to a more regular programme, perhaps conscious that empty days do not necessarily fill up with creative achievement.

Jack Straw's Castle was followed in 1982 by *The Passages of Joy*, a book poised between the open and closed aspects of his poetry. The subjects of *The Passages of Joy* are friendship, pleasure and the passing of time. Gunn was now fifty-three and this was very much the book of a middle-aged man, looking back on past delights and re-evaluating friendships – most, though not all, of the friends being representative of the life of gay men in this new, more open era. The year 1982 also saw the publication of *The Occasions of Poetry: Essays in Criticism and Autobiography*, which included the essay on William Carlos Williams, introductions to Fulke Greville and Ben Jonson, and some pungently condensed essays in autobiography. Eleven years later, a further collection of criticism, *Shelf Life*, contained the finest of his essays, 'What the Slowworm Said', on Ezra Pound, T. S. Eliot and Basil Bunting, as well as articles on Robert Duncan and memoirs of Yvor Winters and Christopher Isherwood. Gunn's criticism is impressive, though modestly framed; it is always accurate and sharply exemplified, but not at all academic. The prose is direct and limpid; he does not theorise but leads the reader through the process of reading poems.

In 1983 the world began to be conscious of a new epidemic. It was called acquired immune deficiency syndrome but quickly came to be known by the acronym AIDS. In the Western world, its most visible victims were sexually active gay men, and San Francisco became the epicentre of what quickly came to be perceived as a real plague. As the plague spread, so did alarm. In 1986 Gunn agreed to care for a close friend dying of the disease. His two-week bedside vigil resulted in the longest continuous poem that he wrote, the 116 lines of 'Lament' (pp. 167–71), a major addition to the great English tradition of pastoral elegy that includes poems by Milton, Shelley and Tennyson. Soon afterwards other friends fell ill and died. One month in 1987 saw the deaths of no fewer than four of Gunn's friends, two of them on the same day. Among them was Charlie Hinkle, a talented young poet in his late twenties with whom Gunn was emotionally and sexually involved. In 'The J Car' (pp. 175–76), he evokes his late meetings with Hinkle as the latter's short life reached its last stage:

> I'd leave him to the feverish sleep ahead,
> Myself to ride through darkened yards instead
> Back to my health. Of course I simplify.
> Of course. It tears me still that he should die
> As only an apprentice to his trade,
> The ultimate engagements not yet made.
> His gifts had been withdrawing one by one
> Even before their usefulness was done:
> This optic nerve would never be relit;
> The other flickered, soon to be with it.
> Unready, disappointed, unachieved,
> He knew he would not write the much-conceived
> Much-hoped-for work now, nor yet help create
> A love he might in full reciprocate.

If Gunn ever rose to an occasion, it was in these poems expressing these dreadful losses. The poems recall the tone of Ben Jonson, master of brief laments and the poetry of friendship. Gunn disliked the Confessional poetry of the 1960s and 1970s, with its emphasis on self-display and self-exposure. The stoical reticence practised by Jonson now gave him the means of writing about his loss without betraying the depths of private feeling or falling into hysteria. As more and more friends died, a string of elegies followed, each of them deeply poignant, the poignancy an effect of the reticence. The achievement is as much moral as literary. The collection containing these poems, *The Man with Night Sweats* (1992), brought about a revival in Gunn's reputation.

Remarkably, Gunn did not himself contract AIDS, though the title poem of *The Man with Night Sweats* evokes his apprehensions in that regard. He began to think of himself as a survivor and death became a major new subject for him. There were not only the AIDS elegies, but the poems he wrote about literary friends – Christopher Isherwood (p. 161) and, later, in his last book, *Boss Cupid* (2000), Robert Duncan (pp. 181–82). Then, in 1991, he finally dealt with the death that had haunted him since the age of fourteen: his mother's. 'The Gas-poker' begins with reflections on the length of time that had passed: 'Forty-eight years ago / – Can it be forty-eight / Since then? – they forced the door . . .' The key word there is 'they'. He at last succeeded in getting the memory down only when it had occurred to him – taking a hint from Thomas Hardy – that it was possible to write in the third person. A slight crankiness to the rhyme scheme and metre also recalls Hardy – in disyllabic rhymes such as 'barricaded'/'they did', for instance. It is by 'closures' of this kind that Gunn succeeds in distancing the experience and, as in the AIDS elegies, it is precisely the note of reticence needed for speech to occur at all that moves the reader, who is forced to imagine for him- or herself the pain that occasioned the poem.

Like the AIDS elegies – and in remoter ways, like 'Misanthropos' and *Moly* – 'The Gas-poker' is a pastoral. The setting is a garden. The 'sort of backwards flute' that fed gas into Charlotte Gunn's mouth is a perversion of the reed or 'oaten stop' of pastoral song. 'Ago' at the end of the first line rhymes with the first lines of each of the four subsequent stanzas, the sequence culminating with 'flow', which evokes the uninterrupted flow of a musical line. The brothers 'Repeating their lament' are not only in the everyday sense a burden to each other, but to quote the line correctly 'A burden, to each other' – that is (in musical terms), 'a chorus or refrain, or the drone of an instrument'. The dead woman is, at the end of the poem, filled up by the poker's 'music' and so 'mute'. Mute, yet alive in her son's songs, whose Muse, giver of music, she had always been.

Reading this poem with its distancing, wit and artistry, it is not difficult to see why Gunn was wary of Confessional poetry. 'I don't like dramatizing myself,' he said in an interview. 'I don't want to be Sylvia Plath' (JC, p. 15). As it happens, he didn't read the last poems of Sylvia Plath until 1965 – two years after her death – when I lent him my copies. When he returned them to me, he wrote this:

> I am still not quite sure what they add up to. Each poem is a series of exclamations and images loosely connected by the themes stated in the title, but the connection is often very loose. Only about two of the poems . . . have any construction worth talking about. The result is that they together make a kind of rambling hysterical monologue, which is fine for people who believe in art as Organic but less satisfactory for those who demand more. Nevertheless there are some incredibly beautiful passages, where an image suddenly emerges from the crowd of other images and <u>takes over</u> for a few lines . . . The trouble is with the emotion, itself, really: it is largely one of hysteria, and it is amazing that her hysteria has produced poetry as good as this. I think there's a tremendous danger in the fact that we <u>know</u> she committed suicide. If they were anonymous poems I wonder how we'd take them.
>
> (CW, 25 February 1965)

What he did not say is that, if he had wanted to be Plath, he had the perfect subject matter ready and waiting. But he didn't believe that dying was an art and his subject hurt too much to permit direct expression.

It is beginning to be clear that Gunn's last two books were

carefully planned as the formal conclusion to his life's work. He may not have been consistent in this plan, but despite the appearance of bohemian spontaneity, he was an orderly man – almost obsessively so – and he had very clear ideas of what he wanted his work to be. Any poem that dissatisfied him he excluded from the books, and each is meticulously shaped. Not long after publishing *The Passages of Joy* in 1982, Gunn told his friends and publishers that he would not be publishing another book for ten years, about twice as long as his usual gap between books. He had always found that, once a new book was out, he would suffer from writer's block for a year or two, so he decided that this time he would not think about a new collection until he was sure he had more than enough poems to select from. In the event, the AIDS elegies, which he could not have anticipated, determined the shape of *The Man with Night Sweats* and there were a few poems left over that found their way into his last book. The opening poem of *Boss Cupid*, 'Duncan', was begun as early as 1988, when he was still involved with writing about AIDS, and it continues the preoccupation with elegy, as does 'The Gas-poker', written a year before the publication of *The Man with Night Sweats*. Everything else one can say about *Boss Cupid* suggests that he knew it would be his last production.

'Duncan' (pp. 181–82) is not just a tribute to a friend and poet but an *ars poetica*. It both describes and exemplifies the interplay of process and formality in Gunn's own poetry. A few pages after it comes 'The Gas-poker', prefaced by 'My Mother's Pride', the two poems suggesting that at last he had managed to come to terms with the love and the tragedy that had shaped his thought and work. The middle section of the book, 'Gossip', is a set of light free-verse poems a little in the manner of Frank O'Hara, a section very much in contrast to the weighty summations and sequences in the last section, though it includes a self-portrait of some beauty: 'The Artist as an Old Man' (pp. 188–89). The final section of the book is a series of poems, heavily influenced by Elizabethan poetry, about love. It is presided over by that very Elizabethan deity, the bullying god Gunn refers to as 'Boss Cupid'. The last section covers all kinds of love, from the paradisal love of Dante for Beatrice to the desires of a serial killer who ate the men he was attracted to. Gunn had never attempted summations before but he does so in this book, and in the final sequence, almost the last thing he wrote, he presents himself as King David dancing before God. The three monologues of 'Dancing David' cover the key periods of David's life, and the book concludes with dancing David taking his final bow: 'A brief bow following on the final leap' (p. 197).

Few of the book's first readers can have guessed that this was to be Gunn's farewell – like Prospero drowning his books. Though Gunn was seventy and had just retired from teaching, he was still energetic and physically fit; he retained his ebullient good nature and sense of fun. But once he had lost the order imposed by a regular job, his habit of self-discipline seemed to fail him. His need for youth, both in himself and in those he encountered sexually, became an affliction. He found that, though he could compose by will, the resulting poems were lifeless: 'I've got no juice,' he told me in 2003, which turned out to be the last time I saw him. For many years he had taken drugs recreationally, but he had always remained conscious of the necessity for rational self-control. To fuel his nights of cruising and leather bars, he now began taking 'speed' or methamphetamine, tremendously dangerous for an elderly man's heart. He knew, or had decided, that his literary life was over, so he felt no need to preserve himself for adventures of the intellect. As we gather from some of the poems in *Boss Cupid*, he became more and more attached to the homeless young gay men who haunted the streets of San Francisco, many of them addicts. Increasingly this became a problem for his housemates. For one thing there was noise off and on throughout the night. For another the boys were hard to communicate with, occasionally robbed Gunn and generally disturbed the life of the house. Gunn himself seemed unconscious of the fact that he was alienating his friends, people he had lived with for half his life – in Kitay's case for two-thirds of it.

On 10 April 2004, his friends heard someone drop by in the early morning. They could hear the television in Gunn's bedroom all day long, so imagined he was in the room with a boy. But no one ever seemed to leave the room. Eventually one friend, Bob Bair, decided to risk a confrontation. He went into the room and found Gunn dead on the floor beside the bed, mouth open and eyes staring. At some stage the boy he had been with must have slipped out into the street. According to the coroner's report, Gunn died of a drug overdose, with methamphetamine, heroin and alcohol in his system.

I tell this story in detail here because it seems so out of character for Thom Gunn. But that is not quite it, exactly. Rather, it shows how he might have led his life but in the event did not. He adored his mother but she killed herself and let him find her body. He continued to make excuses for her until the end, but he must have felt at some level betrayed and abandoned. That feeling shows in the attraction he felt for boys who had been similarly abandoned; as somebody once said to me, he *mothered* those boys. But his mother had left him a way of coping without her. Sharing her love of literature and her respect for it, he found he was able to convert experience into words, rhythms and the 'concord of sweet sounds'. In his work as a poet, as in most of what he did – his teaching, for instance – he was extremely self-disciplined and orderly, but he must have seen that a time would come when he no longer had the energy to sustain a poem or a sexual relationship. He planned his work for as long as he could, and then (long before he needed to have done so) he gave up. In a sense he killed himself, not in an act of willed suicide like his mother's, but by letting himself go, courting death – he always enjoyed risk – and doing it so rashly that at some time, as he must have known, his body would give up the struggle. It was a chosen death, but chosen by a man who had earlier chosen life.

Thom Gunn's reputation peaked early, his first book appearing when he was twenty-four. He was the leather-jacketed, existentialist hero the late 1950s required. But fashion overtook him. He detested the confessional mode, preferring an almost anonymous tone like that of the Elizabethans he loved. His increasing Americanisation lost him much of his English audience, but he never won a wide following in the United States. This did not discourage him. Tall, lean and handsome, he loved posing and dressed at times like a dandyish buccaneer; but he was also rather a modest man, his behaviour marked by consideration for others. He ran the risk, indeed, of underestimating his own importance. But this enabled him to regard the creation of a well-made poem as something that mattered more than his ego did, the result being a body of work more consistently well written than that of any of his contemporaries. He also remembered the lessons he had learnt from his mother and from the poets and teachers he most admired: that poems are concerned with life and that to put an experience truthfully into words is to begin to understand it, the understanding being a moral act. As a result, when his world was shaken by crisis, as it was by AIDS in the 1980s, his art was ready for it.

CLIVE WILMER

SELECTED POEMS

from
FIGHTING TERMS
(1954)

The Wound

The huge wound in my head began to heal
About the beginning of the seventh week.
Its valleys darkened, its villages became still:
For joy I did not move and dared not speak,
Not doctors would cure it, but time, its patient skill.

And constantly my mind returned to Troy.
After I sailed the seas I fought in turn
On both sides, sharing even Helen's joy
Of place, and growing up – to see Troy burn –
As Neoptolemus, that stubborn boy.

I lay and rested as prescription said.
Manoeuvred with the Greeks, or sallied out
Each day with Hector. Finally my bed
Became Achilles' tent, to which the lout
Thersites came reporting numbers dead.

I was myself: subject to no man's breath:
My own commander was my enemy.
And while my belt hung up, sword in the sheath,
Thersites shambled in and breathlessly
Cackled about my friend Patroclus' death.

I called for armour, rose, and did not reel.
But, when I thought, rage at his noble pain
Flew to my head, and turning I could feel
My wound break open wide. Over again
I had to let those storm-lit valleys heal.

Carnal Knowledge

Even in bed I pose: desire may grow
More circumstantial and less circumspect
Each night, but an acute girl would suspect
That my self is not like my body, bare.
I wonder if you know, or, knowing, care?
You know I know you know I know you know.

I am not what I seem, believe me, so
For the magnanimous pagan I pretend
Substitute a forked creature as your friend.
When darkness lies without a roll or stir
Flaccid, you want a competent poseur.
I know you know I know you know I know.

Cackle you hen, and answer when I crow.
No need to grope: I'm still playing the same
Comical act inside the tragic game.
Yet things perhaps are simpler: could it be
A mere tear-jerker void of honesty?
You know I know you know I know you know.

Leave me. Within a minute I will stow
Your greedy mouth, but will not yet to grips.
'There is a space between the breast and lips.'
Also a space between the thighs and head,
So great, we might as well not be in bed.
I know you know I know you know I know.

I hardly hoped for happy thoughts, although
In a most happy sleeping time I dreamt
We did not hold each other in contempt.
Then lifting from my lids night's penny weights
I saw that lack of love contaminates.
You know I know you know I know you know.

Abandon me to stammering, and go;
If you have tears, prepare to cry elsewhere –
I know of no emotion we can share.
Your intellectual protests are a bore
And even now I pose, so now go, for
I know you know.

Lerici

Shelley was drowned near here. Arms at his side
He fell submissive through the waves, and he
Was but a minor conquest of the sea:
The darkness that he met was nurse not bride.

Others make gestures with arms open wide,
Compressing in the minute before death
What great expense of muscle and of breath
They would have made if they had never died.

Byron was worth the sea's pursuit. His touch
Was masterful to water, audience
To which he could react until an end.
Strong swimmers, fishermen, explorers: such
Dignify death by thriftless violence –
Squandering with so little left to spend.

Tamer and Hawk

I thought I was so tough,
But gentled at your hands,
Cannot be quick enough
To fly for you and show
That when I go I go
At your commands.

Even in flight above
I am no longer free:
You seeled me with your love,
I am blind to other birds –
The habit of your words
Has hooded me.

As formerly, I wheel
I hover and I twist,
But only want the feel,
In my possessive thought,
Of catcher and of caught
Upon your wrist.

You but half civilize,
Taming me in this way.
Through having only eyes
For you I fear to lose,
I lose to keep, and choose
Tamer as prey.

Incident on a Journey

One night I reached a cave: I slept, my head
Full of the air. There came about daybreak
A red-coat soldier to the mouth, who said
'I am not living, in hell's pains I ache,
  But I regret nothing.'

His forehead had a bloody wound whose streaming
The pallid staring face illuminated.
Whether his words were mine or his, in dreaming
I found they were my deepest thoughts translated.
  '*I regret nothing*:

'Turn your closed eyes to see upon these walls
A mural scratched there by an earlier man,
And coloured with the blood of animals:
Showing humanity beyond its span,
  Regretting nothing.

'No plausible nostalgia, no brown shame
I had when treating with my enemies.
And always when a living impulse came
I acted, and my action made me wise.
  And I regretted nothing.

'I as possessor of unnatural strength
Was hunted, one day netted in a brawl;
A minute far beyond a minute's length
Took from me passion, strength, and life, and all.
  But I regretted nothing.

'Their triumph left my body in the dust;
The dust and beer still clotting in my hair
When I rise lonely, will-less. Where I must
I go, and what I must I bear.
   And I regret nothing.

'My lust runs yet and is unsatisfied,
My hate throbs yet but I am feeble-limbed;
If as an animal I could have died
My death had scattered instinct to the wind,
   Regrets as nothing.'

Later I woke. I started to my feet.
The valley light, the mist already going.
I was alive and felt my body sweet,
Uncaked blood in all its channels flowing.
   I would regret nothing.

from
THE SENSE OF MOVEMENT
(1957)

On the Move

The blue jay scuffling in the bushes follows
Some hidden purpose, and the gust of birds
That spurts across the field, the wheeling swallows,
Has nested in the trees and undergrowth.
Seeking their instinct, or their poise, or both,
One moves with an uncertain violence
Under the dust thrown by a baffled sense
Or the dull thunder of approximate words.

On motorcycles, up the road, they come:
Small, black, as flies hanging in heat, the Boys,
Until the distance throws them forth, their hum
Bulges to thunder held by calf and thigh.
In goggles, donned impersonality,
In gleaming jackets trophied with the dust,
They strap in doubt – by hiding it, robust –
And almost hear a meaning in their noise.

Exact conclusion of their hardiness
Has no shape yet, but from known whereabouts
They ride, direction where the tyres press.
They scare a flight of birds across the field:
Much that is natural, to the will must yield.
Men manufacture both machine and soul,
And use what they imperfectly control
To dare a future from the taken routes.

It is a part solution, after all.
One is not necessarily discord
On earth; or damned because, half animal,
One lacks direct instinct, because one wakes
Afloat on movement that divides and breaks.
One joins the movement in a valueless world,
Choosing it, till, both hurler and the hurled,
One moves as well, always toward, toward.

A minute holds them, who have come to go:
The self-defined, astride the created will
They burst away; the towns they travel through
Are home for neither bird nor holiness,
For birds and saints complete their purposes.
At worst, one is in motion; and at best,
Reaching no absolute, in which to rest,
One is always nearer by not keeping still.

At the Back of the North Wind

All summer's warmth was stored there in the hay;
Below, the troughs of water froze: the boy
Climbed nightly up the rungs behind the stalls
And planted deep between the clothes he heard
The kind wind bluster, but the last he knew
Was sharp and filled his head, the smell of hay.

Here wrapped within the cobbled mews he woke.
Passing from summer, climbing down through winter
He broke into an air that kept no season:
Denying change, for it was always there.
It nipped the memory numb, scalding away
The castle of winter and the smell of hay.

The ostlers knew, but did not tell him more
Than hay is what we turn to. Other smells,
Horses, leather, manure, fresh sweat, and sweet
Mortality, he found them on the North.
That was her sister, East, that shrilled all day
And swept the mews dead clean from wisps of hay.

Autumn Chapter in a Novel

Through woods, Mme Une Telle, a trifle ill
With idleness, but no less beautiful,
Walks with the young tutor, round their feet
Mob syllables slurred to a fine complaint,
Which in their time held off the natural heat.

The sun is distant, and they fill out space
Sweatless as watercolour under glass.
He kicks abruptly. But we may suppose
The leaves he scatters thus will settle back
In much the same position as they rose.

A tutor's indignation works on air,
Altering nothing; action bustles where,
Towards the pool by which they lately stood,
The husband comes discussing with his bailiff
Poachers, the broken fences round the wood.

Pighead! The poacher is at large, and lingers,
A dead mouse gripped between his sensitive fingers:
Fences already keep the live game out:
See how your property twists her parasol,
Hesitates in the tender trap of doubt.

Here they repair, here daily handle lightly
The brief excitements that disturb them nightly;
Sap draws back inch by inch, and to the ground
The words they uttered rustle constantly:
Silent, they watch the growing, weightless mound.

They leave at last a chosen element,
Resume the motions of their discontent;
She takes her sewing up, and he again
Names to her son the deserts on the globe,
And leaves thrust violently upon the pane.

The Silver Age

Do not enquire from the centurion nodding
At the corner, with his head gentle over
The swelling breastplate, where true Rome is found.
Even of Livy there are volumes lost.
All he can do is guide you through the moonlight.

When he moves, mark how his eager striding,
To which we know the darkness is a river
Sullen with mud, is easy as on ground.
We know it is a river never crossed
By any but some few who hate the moonlight.

And when he speaks, mark how his ancient wording
Is hard with indignation of a lover.
'I do not think our new Emperor likes the sound
Of turning squadrons or the last post.
Consorts with Christians, I think he lives in moonlight.'

Hurrying to show you his companions guarding,
He grips your arm like a cold strap of leather,
Then halts, earthpale, as he stares round and round.
What made this one fragment of a sunken coast
Remain, far out, to be beaten by the moonlight?

Elvis Presley

Two minutes long it pitches through some bar:
Unreeling from a corner box, the sigh
Of this one, in his gangling finery
And crawling sideburns, wielding a guitar.

The limitations where he found success
Are ground on which he, panting, stretches out
In turn, promiscuously, by every note.
Our idiosyncrasy and our likeness.

We keep ourselves in touch with a mere dime:
Distorting hackneyed words in hackneyed songs
He turns revolt into a style, prolongs
The impulse to a habit of the time.

Whether he poses or is real, no cat
Bothers to say: the pose held is a stance,
Which, generation of the very chance
It wars on, may be posture for combat.

The Allegory of the Wolf Boy

The causes are in Time; only their issue
Is bodied in the flesh, the finite powers.
And how to guess he hides in that firm tissue
Seeds of division? At tennis and at tea
Upon the gentle lawn, he is not ours,
But plays us in a sad duplicity.

Tonight the boy, still boy open and blond,
Breaks from the house, wedges his clothes between
Two moulded garden urns, and goes beyond
His understanding, through the dark and dust:
Fields of sharp stubble, abandoned by machine
To the whirring enmity of insect lust.

As yet ungolden in the dense, hot night
The spikes enter his feet: he seeks the moon,
Which, with the touch of its infertile light,
Shall loose desires hoarded against his will
By the long urging of the afternoon.
Slowly the hard rim shifts above the hill.

White in the beam he stops, faces it square,
And the same instant leaping from the ground
Feels the familiar itch of close dark hair;
Then, clean exception to the natural laws,
Only to instinct and the moon being bound,
Drops on four feet. Yet he has bleeding paws.

Jesus and his Mother

My only son, more God's than mine,
Stay in this garden ripe with pears.
The yielding of their substance wears
A modest and contented shine:
And when they weep with age, not brine
But lazy syrup are their tears.
'I am my own and not my own.'

He seemed much like another man,
That silent foreigner who trod
Outside my door with lily rod:
How could I know what I began
Meeting the eyes more furious than
The eyes of Joseph, those of God?
I was my own and not my own.

And who are these twelve labouring men?
I do not understand your words:
I taught you speech, we named the birds,
You marked their big migrations then
Like any child. So turn again
To silence from the place of crowds.
'I am my own and not my own.'

Why are you sullen when I speak?
Here are your tools, the saw and knife
And hammer on your bench. Your life
Is measured here in week and week
Planed as the furniture you make,
And I will teach you like a wife
To be my own and all my own.

Who like an arrogant wind blown
Where he may please, needs no content?
Yet I remember how you went
To speak with scholars in furred gown.
I hear an outcry in the town;
Who carried that dark instrument?
'One all his own and not his own.'

Treading the green and nimble sward
I stare at a strange shadow thrown.
Are you the boy I bore alone,
No doctor near to cut the cord?
I cannot reach to call you Lord,
Answer me as my only son.
'I am my own and not my own.'

To Yvor Winters, 1955

I leave you in your garden.
                              In the yard
Behind it, run the Airedales you have reared
With boxer's vigilance and poet's rigour:
Dog-generations you have trained the vigour
That few can breed to train and fewer still
Control with the deliberate human will.
And in the house there rest, piled shelf on shelf,
The accumulations that compose the self –
Poem and history: for if we use
Words to maintain the actions that we choose,
Our words, with slow defining influence,
Stay to mark out our chosen lineaments.

Continual temptation waits on each
To renounce his empire over thought and speech,
Till he submit his passive faculties
To evening, come where no resistance is;
The unmotivated sadness of the air
Filling the human with his own despair.
Where now lies power to hold the evening back?
Implicit in the grey is total black:
Denial of the discriminating brain
Brings the neurotic vision, and the vein
Of necromancy. All as relative
For mind as for the sense, we have to live
In a half-world, not ours nor history's,
And learn the false from half-true premisses.

But sitting in the dusk – though shapes combine,
Vague mass replacing edge and flickering line,
You keep both Rule and Energy in view,
Much power in each, most in the balanced two:
Ferocity existing in the fence
Built by an exercised intelligence.
Though night is always close, complete negation
Ready to drop on wisdom and emotion,
Night from the air or the carnivorous breath,
Still it is right to know the force of death,
And, as you do, persistent, tough in will,
Raise from the excellent the better still.

Vox Humana

Being without quality
I appear to you at first
as an unkempt smudge, a blur,
an indefinite haze, mere-
ly pricking the eyes, almost
nothing. Yet you perceive me.

I have been always most close
when you had least resistance,
falling asleep, or in bars;
during the unscheduled hours,
though strangely without substance,
I hang, there and ominous.

Aha, sooner or later
you will have to name me, and,
as you name, I shall focus,
I shall become more precise.
O Master (for you command
in naming me, you prefer)!

I was, for Alexander,
the certain victory; I
was hemlock for Socrates;
and, in the dry night, Brutus
waking before Philippi
stopped me, crying out 'Caesar!'

Or if you call me the blur
that in fact I am, you shall
yourself remain blurred, hanging
like smoke indoors. For you bring,
to what you define now, all
there is, ever, of future.

from
MY SAD CAPTAINS
(1961)

In Santa Maria del Popolo

Waiting for when the sun an hour or less
Conveniently oblique makes visible
The painting on one wall of this recess
By Caravaggio, of the Roman School,
I see how shadow in the painting brims
With a real shadow, drowning all shapes out
But a dim horse's haunch and various limbs,
Until the very subject is in doubt.

But evening gives the act, beneath the horse
And one indifferent groom, I see him sprawl,
Foreshortened from the head, with hidden face,
Where he has fallen, Saul becoming Paul.
O wily painter, limiting the scene
From a cacophony of dusty forms
To the one convulsion, what is it you mean
In that wide gesture of the lifting arms?

No Ananias croons a mystery yet,
Casting the pain out under name of sin.
The painter saw what was, an alternate
Candour and secrecy inside the skin.
He painted, elsewhere, that firm insolent
Young whore in Venus' clothes, those pudgy cheats,
Those sharpers; and was strangled, as things went,
For money, by one such picked off the streets.

I turn, hardly enlightened, from the chapel
To the dim interior of the church instead,
In which there kneel already several people,
Mostly old women: each head closeted
In tiny fists holds comfort as it can.
Their poor arms are too tired for more than this
– For the large gesture of solitary man,
Resisting, by embracing, nothingness.

Innocence

to Tony White

He ran the course and as he ran he grew,
And smelt his fragrance in the field. Already,
Running he knew the most he ever knew,
The egotism of a healthy body.

Ran into manhood, ignorant of the past:
Culture of guilt and guilt's vague heritage,
Self-pity and the soul; what he possessed
Was rich, potential, like the bud's tipped rage.

The Corps developed, it was plain to see,
Courage, endurance, loyalty and skill
To a morale firm as morality,
Hardening him to an instrument, until

The finitude of virtues that were there
Bodied within the swarthy uniform
A compact innocence, child-like and clear,
No doubt could penetrate, no act could harm.

When he stood near the Russian partisan
Being burned alive, he therefore could behold
The ribs wear gently through the darkening skin
And sicken only at the Northern cold,

Could watch the fat burn with a violet flame
And feel disgusted only at the smell,
And judge that all pain finishes the same
As melting quietly by his boots it fell.

Modes of Pleasure

New face, strange face, for my unrest.
I hunt your look, and lust marks time
Dark in his doubtful uniform,
Preparing once more for the test.

You do not know you are observed:
Apart, contained, you wait on chance,
Or seem to, till your callous glance
Meets mine, as callous and reserved.

And as it does we recognize
That sharing an anticipation
Amounts to a collaboration –
A warm game for a warmer prize.

Yet when I've had you once or twice
I may not want you any more:
A single night is plenty for
Every magnanimous device.

Why should that matter? Why pretend
Love must accompany erection?
This is a momentary affection,
A curiosity bound to end,

Which as good-humoured muscle may
Against the muscle try its strength
– Exhausted into sleep at length –
And will not last long into day.

[35]

The Byrnies

The heroes paused upon the plain.
When one of them but swayed, ring mashed on ring:
  Sound of the byrnie's knitted chain,
Vague evocations of the constant Thing.

  They viewed beyond a salty hill
Barbaric forest, mesh of branch and root
   – A huge obstruction growing still,
Darkening the land, in quietness absolute.

  That dark was fearful – lack of presence –
Unless some man could chance upon or win
   Magical signs to stay the essence
Of the broad light that they adventured in.

  Elusive light of light that went
Flashing on water, edging round a mass,
   Inching across fat stems, or spent
Lay thin and shrunk among the bristling grass.

  Creeping from sense to craftier sense,
Acquisitive, and loss their only fear,
   These men had fashioned a defence
Against the nicker's snap, and hostile spear.

Byrnie on byrnie! as they turned
They saw light trapped between the man-made joints,
    Central in every link it burned,
Reduced and steadied to a thousand points.

    Thus for each blunt-faced ignorant one
The great grey rigid uniform combined
    Safety with virtue of the sun.
Thus concepts linked like chainmail in the mind.

    Reminded, by the grinding sound,
Of what they sought, and partly understood,
    They paused upon the open ground,
A little group above the foreign wood.

Claus von Stauffenberg

of the bomb-plot on Hitler, 1944

What made the place a landscape of despair,
History stunned beneath, the emblems cracked?
Smell of approaching snow hangs on the air;
The frost meanwhile can be the only fact.

They chose the unknown, and the bounded terror,
As a corrective, who corrected live
Surveying without choice the bounding error:
An unsanctioned present must be primitive.

A few still have the vigour to deny
Fear is a natural state; their motives neither
Of doctrinaire, of turncoat, nor of spy.
Lucidity of thought draws them together.

The maimed young Colonel who can calculate
On two remaining fingers and a will,
Takes lessons from the past, to detonate
A bomb that Brutus rendered possible.

Over the maps a moment, face to face:
Across from Hitler, whose grey eyes have filled
A nation with the illogic of their gaze,
The rational man is poised, to break, to build.

And though he fails, honour personified
In a cold time where honour cannot grow,
He stiffens, like a statue, in mid-stride
– Falling toward history, and under snow.

Flying Above California

Spread beneath me it lies – lean upland
sinewed and tawny in the sun, and

valley cool with mustard, or sweet with
loquat. I repeat under my breath

names of places I have not been to:
Crescent City, San Bernardino

– Mediterranean and Northern names.
Such richness can make you drunk. Sometimes

on fogless days by the Pacific,
there is a cold hard light without break

that reveals merely what is – no more
and no less. That limiting candour,

that accuracy of the beaches,
is part of the ultimate richness.

Considering the Snail

The snail pushes through a green
night, for the grass is heavy
with water and meets over
the bright path he makes, where rain
has darkened the earth's dark. He
moves in a wood of desire,

pale antlers barely stirring
as he hunts. I cannot tell
what power is at work, drenched there
with purpose, knowing nothing.
What is a snail's fury? All
I think is that if later

I parted the blades above
the tunnel and saw the thin
trail of broken white across
litter, I would never have
imagined the slow passion
to that deliberate progress.

The Feel of Hands

The hands explore tentatively,
two small live entities whose shapes
I have to guess at. They touch me
all, with the light of fingertips

testing each surface of each thing
found, timid as kittens with it.
I connect them with amusing
hands I have shaken by daylight.

There is a sudden transition:
they plunge together in a full
formed single fury; they are grown
to cats, hunting without scruple;

they are expert but desperate.
I am in the dark. I wonder
when they grew up. It strikes me that
I do not know whose hands they are.

My Sad Captains

One by one they appear in
the darkness: a few friends, and
a few with historical
names. How late they start to shine!
but before they fade they stand
perfectly embodied, all

the past lapping them like a
cloak of chaos. They were men
who, I thought, lived only to
renew the wasteful force they
spent with each hot convulsion.
They remind me, distant now.

True, they are not at rest yet,
but now that they are indeed
apart, winnowed from failures,
they withdraw to an orbit
and turn with disinterested
hard energy, like the stars.

UNCOLLECTED
(1960s)

From an Asian Tent

Alexander thinks of his father

Father, I scarcely could believe you dead.
The pelts, fur trophies, and hacked skulls that you
Drunkenly hooked up while the bone still bled
I pulled down, and I hung the place instead
With emblems of an airy Hellene blue.

You held me once before the army's eyes;
During their endless shout, I tired and slid
Down past your forearms to the cold surprise
Your plated shoulder made between my thighs.
This happened. Or perhaps I wish it did.

Remembering that you never reached the East,
I have made it mine to the obscurest temple;
Yet each year look more like the man I least
Choose to resemble, bully, drunk, and beast.
Are you a warning, Father, or an example?

from
POSITIVES
(1965)

The Old Woman

Something approaches, about
which she has heard a good deal.
Her deaf ears have caught it, like
a silence in the wainscot
by her head. Her flesh has felt
a chill in her feet, a draught
in her groin. She has watched it
like moonlight on the frayed wood
stealing toward her
floorboard by floorboard. Will it hurt?

Let it come, it is
the terror of full repose,
and so no terror.

from
TOUCH
(1967)

The Goddess

When eyeless fish meet her on
her way upward, they gently
turn together in the dark
brooks. But naked and searching
as a wind, she will allow
no hindrance, none, and bursts up

through potholes and narrow flues
seeking an outlet. Unslowed
by fire, rock, water or clay,
she after a time reaches
the soft abundant soil, which
still does not dissipate her

force – for look! sinewy thyme
reeking in the sunlight; rats
breeding, breeding, in their nests;
and the soldier by a park
bench with his greatcoat collar
up, waiting all evening for

a woman, any woman
her dress tight across her ass
as bark in moonlight. Goddess,
Proserpina: it is we,
vulnerable, quivering,
who stay you to abundance.

Touch

You are already
asleep. I lower
myself in next to
you, my skin slightly
numb with the restraint
of habits, the patina of
self, the black frost
of outsideness, so that even
unclothed it is
a resilient chilly
hardness, a superficially
malleable, dead
rubbery texture.

You are a mound
of bedclothes, where the cat
in sleep braces
its paws against your
calf through the blankets,
and kneads each paw in turn.

Meanwhile and slowly
I feel a is it
my own warmth surfacing or
the ferment of your whole
body that in darkness beneath
the cover is stealing
bit by bit to break
down that chill.

You turn and
hold me tightly, do
you know who
I am or am I
your mother or
the nearest human being to
hold on to in a
dreamed pogrom.

What I, now loosened,
sink into is an old
big place, it is
there already, for
you are already
there, and the cat
got there before you, yet
it is hard to locate.
What is more, the place is
not found but seeps
from our touch in
continuous creation, dark
enclosing cocoon round
ourselves alone, dark
wide realm where we
walk with everyone.

Misanthropos

to Tony Tanner and Don Doody

The Last Man

I

He avoids the momentous rhythm
of the sea, one hill suffices him
who has the entire world to choose from.

He melts through the brown and green silence
inspecting his traps, is lost in dense
thicket, or appears among great stones.

He builds no watch tower. He lives like
the birds, self-contained they hop and peck;
he could conceal himself for a week;

and he learns like them to keep movement
on the undipped wing of the present.
But sometimes when he wakes, with the print

of stone in his side, a relentless
memory of monstrous battle is
keener than counsel of the senses.

He opens, then, a disused channel
to the onset of hatred, until
the final man walks the final hill

without thought or feeling, as before.
If he preserves himself in nature,
it is as a lived caricature

of the race he happens to survive.
He is clothed in dirt. He lacks motive.
He is wholly representative.

II

At last my shout is answered! Are you near,
Man whom I cannot see but can hear?

Here.

The canyon hides you well, which well defended.
Sir, tell me, is the long war ended?

Ended.

I passed no human on my trip, a slow one.
Is it your luck, down there, to know one?

No one.

What have I left, who stood among mankind,
When the firm base is undermined?

A mind.

Yet, with a vacant landscape as its mirror,
What can it choose, to ease the terror?

Error.

Is there no feeling, then, that I can trust,
In spite of what we have discussed?

                                        Disgust.

                    III
Earlier, travelling on the roads where grass
Softened the gutters for the marsh bird's nest,
He walked barefoot already, and already
His uniform was peeling from his back.
And coming to this hill across the plain,
He sloughed it bit by bit. Now that, alone,
He cannot seek himself as messenger,
Or bear dispatches between elm and oak,
It is a clumsy frock he starts to fashion
From skins of mole and rabbit; he considers
That one who wears it is without a role.
But the curled darling who survives the war
Has merely lost the admirers of those curls
That always lavished most warmth on his neck;
Though no one sees him, though it is the wind
Utters ambiguous orders from the plain,
Though nodding foxgloves are his only girls,
His poverty is a sort of uniform.
With a bone needle he pursues himself,
Stitching the patchwork spread across his lap,
A courier after identity, and sees
A pattern grow among the disarray.

IV

The moon appears, distinct where all is dim,
   And steady in the orbit it must go.
   He lies in shadow, then light reaches him.
While, there! the Milky Way follows below,
   A luminous field that swings across the sky.
   The ancient rhythm almost comforts, slow
Bright mild recurrence that he might move by,
   Obedient in the act of breath, and lit,
   Mere life, by matter travelling sure and high.
But this is envy for the inanimate,
   The youth of things. On the dead globe he sees
   Markings as one might on the earth from it,
Where relics of emergent matter freeze.
   Down here, two more births followed on the first:
   Life, consciousness, like linked catastrophes.
Their sequence in him cannot be reversed
   Except in death, thus, when the features set.
   Meanwhile, he must live, as he looks, immersed
In consciousness that plots its own end yet;
   And since the plotter through success would lose
   Knowledge of it, he must without regret
Accept the inheritance he did not choose,
   As he accepted drafting for that war
   That was not of his choosing. He must use
The heaviness, the flaw, he always bore.
   The imperfect moon swims forward on its course;
   Yet, bathed by shade now, he imagines more –
   The clearest light in the whole universe.

V

Green overtaking green, it's
endless; squat grasses creep up,
briars cross, heavily weighed
branches overhang, thickets
crowd in on the brown earth gap
in green which is the path made

by his repeated tread, which,
enacting the wish to move,
is defined by avoidance
of loose ground, of rock and ditch,
of thorn-brimmed hollows, and of
poisoned beds. The ground hardens.

Bare within limits. The trick
is to stay free within them.
The path branches, branches still,
returning to itself, like
a discovering system,
or process made visible.

It rains. He climbs up the hill.
Drops are isolate on leaves,
big and clear. It is cool, and
he breathes the barbarous smell
of the wet earth. Nothing moves
at the edges of the mind.

Memoirs of the World

VI

It has turned cold. I have been gathering wood,
Numb-fingered, hardly feeling what I touched,
Turning crisp leaves to pick up where I could
The damp sticks from beneath them. I have crouched
Piling them up to dry, all afternoon,
And have heard all afternoon, over and over,
Two falling notes – a sweet disconsolate tune,
As if the bird called, from its twiggy cover,
        Nót now, nót now, not now.

I dislodge sticks for kindling, one by one,
From brambles. Struck by shade, I stand and see,
Half blinding me, the cold red setting sun
Through the meshed branches of a leafless tree.
It calls old sunsets to my mind, one most
Which coloured, similarly, the white-grey, blackened
Iron and slabbed concrete of a sentry post
With its cold orange. Let me live, one second,
        Nót now, nót now, not now.

Most poignant and most weakening, that recall.
Although I lived from day to day, too, there.
Yet the comparison makes me sensible
Of the diminishing warmth and light, which were,
Or seem to have been, diminished less than now.
The bird stops. Hardening in the single present,
I know, hearing wind rattle in a bough,
I have always harked thus after an incessant
       Nót now, nót now, nót now.

VII

    Who was it in dark glasses?
    Nobody in the street could
    see if my eyes were open.
    I took them off for movies
    and sleep. I waited, I stood
    an armed angel among men.

    Between the dart of colours
    I wore a darkening and
    perceived an exact structure,
    a chart of the world. The coarse
    menace of line was deepened,
    and light was slightly impure.

Yet as I lingered there was,
I noticed, continual
and faint, an indecision,
a hunger in the senses.
I would devour the thin wail
of foghorns, or abandon

my whole self time after time
to the chipped glossy surface
of some doorjamb, for instance,
cramming my nail with its grime,
stroking humps where colourless
paint had filled faults to substance.

I was presence without full
being: from the streetcorner,
in the mere fact of movement,
was I entering the role
of spy or spied on, master
or the world's abject servant?

VIII

Dryads, reposing in the bark's hard silence,
Circled about the edges of my fire,
Exact in being, absolute in balance,
Instruct me how to find here my desire:

To separate the matter from its burning,
Where, in the flux that your composures lack,
Each into other constantly is turning.
In the glowing fall of ash – rose, grey, and black,

I search for meaning, studying to remember
What the world was, and meant. Therefore I try
To reconstruct it in a dying ember,
And wonder, does fire make it live or die?

And evil everywhere or nowhere, stealing
Out of my reach, on air, shows like a spark.
I think I grasp it. The momentary feeling
Is merely pain, evil's external mark.

The neighbouring cinders redden now together,
Like earlier worlds to search, where I am shown
Only myself, although I seek another,
A man who burnt from sympathy alone.

IX

A serving man. Curled my hair,
wore gloves in my cap. I served
all degrees and both sexes.
But I gave readily from
the largess of high spirits,
a sturdy body and strong

fingers. Nor was I servile.
No passer-by could resist
the fragrant impulse nodding
upon my smile. I laboured
to become a god of charm,
an untirable giver.

Needing me, needing me, 'Quick!'
they would call: I came gladly.
Even as I served them sweets
I served myself a trencher
of human flesh in some dark
sour pantry, and munched from it.

My diet, now, is berries,
water, and the gristle of
rodents. I brought myself here,
widening the solitude
till it was absolute. But
at times I am ravenous.

x

All that snow pains my eyes, but I stare
on, stare on, lying in my shelter,

feverish, out at the emptiness.
A negative of matter, it is

a dead white surface at random crossed
by thin twigs and bird tracks on the crust

like fragments of black netting: hard, cold,
windswept. But now my mind loses hold

and, servant to an unhinged body,
becoming of it, sinks rapidly

beneath the stitched furs I'm swaddled in,
beneath the stink of my trembling skin,

till it enters the heart of fever,
as its captive, unable to stir.

I watch the cells swimming in concert
like nebulae, calm, without effort,

great clear globes, pink and white. – But look at
the intruder with blurred outline that

glides in among the shoals, colourless,
with tendrils like an anemone's

drifting all around it like long fur,
gently, unintelligently. Where

it touches it holds, in an act of
enfolding, possessing, merging love.

There is coupling where no such should be.
Surely it is a devil, surely

it is life's parody I see, which
enthrals a universe with its rich

heavy passion, leaving behind it
gorgeous mutations only, then night.

It ends. I open my eyes to snow.
I can sleep now; as I drowse I know

I must keep to the world's bare surface,
I must perceive, and perceive what is:

for though the hold of perception must
harden but diminish, like the frost,

yet still there may be something retained
against the inevitable end.

XI
Epitaph for Anton Schmidt

The Schmidts obeyed, and marched on Poland.
And there an Anton Schmidt, Feldwebel,
Performed uncommon things, not safe,
Nor glamorous, nor profitable.

Was the expression on his face
'Reposeful and humane good nature'?
Or did he look like any Schmidt,
Of slow and undisclosing feature?

I know he had unusual eyes,
Whose power no orders might determine,
Not to mistake the men he saw,
As others did, for gods or vermin.

For five months, till his execution,
Aware that action has its dangers,
He helped the Jews to get away
– Another race at that, and strangers.

He never did mistake for bondage
The military job, the chances,
The limits; he did not submit
To the blackmail of his circumstances.

I see him in the Polish snow,
His muddy wrappings small protection,
Breathing the cold air of his freedom
And treading a distinct direction.

Elegy on the Dust

XII

The upper slopes are busy with the cricket;
  But downhill, hidden in the thicket,
Birds alternate with sudden piercing calls
  The rustling from small animals
Retreating, venturing, as they hunt and breed
  Interdependent in that shade.

Beneath it, glare and silence cow the brain
  Where, troughed between the hill and plain,
The expanse of dust waits: acres calm and deep,
  Swathes folded on themselves in sleep
Or waves that, as if frozen in mid-roll,
  Hang in ridged rows. They cannot fall,
Yet imperceptibly they shift, at flood,
  In quiet encroachment on the wood –
First touching stalk and leaf with silvery cast,
  They block the pores to death at last
And drift in silky banks around the trunk,
  Where dock and fern are fathoms sunk.

Yet farther from the hill the bowl of dust
  Is open to the casual gust
That dives upon its silence, teasing it
  Into a spasm of wild grit.
Here it lies unprotected from the plain,
  And vexed with constant loss and gain,
It seems, of the world's refuse and debris,
  Turns to a vaguely heaving sea,
Where its own eddies, spouts, and calms appear.
  But seas contain a graveyard: here
The graveyard is the sea, material things
  – From stone to claw, scale, pelt, and wings –
Are all reduced to one form and one size.
  And here the human race, too, lies.
An imperfection endlessly refined
  By the imperfection of the mind.
They have all come who sought distinction hard
  To this universal knacker's yard,
Blood dried, flesh shrivelled, and bone decimated:
  Motion of life is thus repeated,
A process ultimately without pain
  As they are broken down again.
The remnants of their guilt mix as they must
  And average out in grains of dust
Too light to act, too small to harm, too fine
  To simper or betray or whine.

Each colourless hard grain is now distinct,
    In no way to its neighbour linked,
Yet from wind's unpremeditated labours
    It drifts in concord with its neighbours,
Perfect community in its behaviour.
    It yields to what it sought, a saviour:
Scattered and gathered, irregularly blown,
    Now sheltered by a ridge or stone,
Now lifted on strong upper winds, and hurled
    In endless hurry round the world.

The First Man

XIII

The present is a secure place to inhabit,
The past being fallen from the mind, the future
A repetition, only, with variations:
The same mouse on its haunches, nibbling, absorbed,
Another piece of root between the forefeet
Slender as wishbones; the woodlice, silvery balls;
The leaves still falling in vestiges of light.

Is he a man? If man is cogitation,
This is at most a rudimentary man,
An unreflecting organ of perception;
Slow as a bull, in moving; yet, in taking,
Quick as an adder. He does not dream at night.

Echo is in the past, the snow long past,
The year has recovered and put forth many times.

He is bent, looks smaller, and is furred, it seems.
Molelike he crouches over mounds of dirt,
Sifting. His eyes have sunk behind huge brows.
His nostrils twitch, distinguishing one by one
The smells of the unseen that blend to make
The black smell of the earth, smell of the Mother,
Smell of her food: pale tender smell of worms,
Tough sweet smell of her roots. He is a nose.
He picks through the turned earth, and eats. A mouth.

If he is man, he is the first man lurking
In a thicket of time. The mesh of green grows tighter.
There is yew, and oak picked out with mistletoe.
Watch, he is darkening in the heavy shade
Of trunks that thicken in the ivy's grip.

XIV
  'What is it? What?'
Mouth struggles with the words that mind forgot.
    While from the high brown swell
He watches it, the smudge, he sees it grow
As it crawls closer, crawls unturnable
And unforeseen upon the plain below.

'That must be men.'
Knowledge invades him, yet he shrinks again
   And sickens to live still
Upon the green slopes of his isolation,
The 'final man upon a final hill,'
As if he did a sort of expiation.

   And now he dreams
Of a shadowed pool nearby fed by two streams:
   If he washed there, he might,
Skin tautened from the chill, emerge above,
Inhuman as a star, as cold, as white,
Freed from all dust. And yet he does not move.

   Could he assert
To men who climb up in their journey's dirt
   That clean was separate?
The dirt would dry back, hardening in the heat:
Perpetual that unease, that world of grit
Breathed in, and gathered on the hands and feet.

   He is unaware
Of the change already taking place as there,
   In the cold clear early light
He, lingering on the scorched grass wet with dew,
Still hunched but now a little more upright,
In picturing man almost becomes man too.

XV

Hidden behind a rock, he watches, grown
As stony as a lizard poised on stone.
Below, the indeterminate shape flows steady
From plain to wood, from wood to slope. Already
Sharp outlines break, in movement, from the edge.
Then in approach upon the final ridge
It is slowly lost to sight, but he can hear
The shingle move with feet. Then they appear,
Being forty men and women, twos and threes,
Over the rim. From where he is he sees
One of the last men stumble, separate,
Up to the rock, this rock, and lean on it.
You can hear him gulp for wind, he is so close,
You can hear his hand rasp on the shrivelled moss
Blotching the rock: by peering you can see
What a ribbed bony creature it must be,
Sweat streaking dirt at collarbones and spine,
Sores round the mouth disfiguring the line.

And on the thin chest two long parallel
Clear curving scratches are discernible.
Recent, for only now the drops within
Steal through the white torn edges of the skin
To mix with dirt. Round here, such cuts are common.
It is not hard to visualize the human,
Tired, walking upward on a wooded slant;
Keeping his eyes upon the ground in front,
He made his way round some dropped rotten limb,

And a hanging briar unnoticed swung at him.
And only later does it start to sting.
That wood has its own way of countering.
The watcher is disturbed, not knowing why.
He has with obstinate equanimity,
Unmoving and unmoved, watched all the rest,
But seeing the trivial scratches on the chest,
He frowns. And he performs an action next
So unconsidered that he is perplexed,
Even in performing it, by what it means –
He walks around to where the creature leans.
The creature sees him, jumps back, staggers, calls,
Then, losing balance on the pebbles, falls.

Now that he has moved toward, through, and beyond
The impulse he does not yet understand,
He must continue where he has begun,
Finding, as when a cloud slips from the sun,
He has entered, without stirring, on a field
The same and yet more green and more detailed,
Each act of growth discovered by his gaze;
Yet if the place is changed by what surveys,
He is surveyed and he himself is changed,
Bombarded by perceptions, rearranged –
Rays on the skin investing with a shape,
A clarity he cannot well escape.

He stops, bewildered by his force, and then
Lifts up the other to his feet again.

XVI

Others approach, and I grip
his arm. For it seems to me
they file past my mind, my mind
perched on this bare rock, watching.

They turn and look at me full,
and as they pass they name me.

What is the name Adam speaks
after the schedule of beasts?

Though I grip his arm, the man,
the scratched man, seems among them,
and as he pauses the old
bitter dizziness hits me:
I almost fall. The stale stench!
the hangdog eyes, the pursed mouth!
no hero or saint, that one.

It is a bare world, and lacks
history; I am neither
his lord nor his servant.

By an act of memory,
I make the recognition:
I stretch out the word to him
from which conversations start,
naming him, also, by name.

XVII

Others approach. Well, this one may show trust
    Around whose arm his fingers fit.
The touched arm feels of dust, mixing with dust
        On the hand that touches it.

And yet a path is dust, or it is none,
    – Merely unstable mud, or weeds,
Or a stream that quietly slips on and on
        Through the undergrowth it feeds.

His own flesh, which he hardly feels, feels dust
    Raised by the war both partly caused
And partly fought, and yet survived. You must,
        If you can, pause; and, paused,

Turn out toward others, meeting their look at full,
    Until you have completely stared
On all there is to see. Immeasurable,
        The dust yet to be shared.

Pierce Street

Nobody home. Long threads of sunlight slant
Past curtains, blind, and slat, through the warm room.
The beams are dazzling, but, random and scant,
Pierce where they end
                small areas of the gloom
On curve of chairleg or a green stalk's bend.

I start exploring. Beds and canvases
Are shapes in each room off the corridor,
Their colours muted, square thick presences
Rising between
              the ceiling and the floor,
A furniture inferred much more than seen.

Here in the seventh room my search is done.
A bluefly circles, irregular and faint.
And round the wall above me friezes run:
Fixed figures drawn
             in charcoal or in paint.
Out of night now the flesh-tint starts to dawn.

Some stand there as if muffled from the cold,
Some naked in it, the wind around a roof.
But armed, their holsters as if tipped with gold.
And twice life-size –
            in line, in groups, aloof,
They all stare down with large abstracted eyes.

A silent garrison, and always there,
They are the soldiers of the imagination
Produced by it to guard it everywhere.
Bodied within
              the limits of their station
As, also, I am bodied in my skin,

They vigilantly preserve as they prevent
And are the thing they guard, having some time stood
Where the painter reached to make them permanent.
The floorboards creak.
                  The house smells of its wood.
Those who are transitory can move and speak.

from
MOLY
(1971)

Rites of Passage

Something is taking place.
Horns bud bright in my hair.
My feet are turning hoof.
And Father, see my face
– Skin that was damp and fair
Is barklike and, feel, rough.

See Greytop how I shine.
I rear, break loose, I neigh
Snuffing the air, and harden
Toward a completion, mine.
And next I make my way
Adventuring through your garden.

My play is earnest now.
I canter to and fro.
My blood, it is like light.
Behind an almond bough,
Horns gaudy with its snow,
I wait live, out of sight.

All planned before my birth
For you, Old Man, no other,
Whom your groin's trembling warns.
I stamp upon the earth
A message to my mother.
And then I lower my horns.

Moly

Nightmare of beasthood, snorting, how to wake.
I woke. What beasthood skin she made me take?

Leathery toad that ruts for days on end,
Or cringing dribbling dog, man's servile friend,

Or cat that prettily pounces on its meat,
Tortures it hours, then does not care to eat:

Parrot, moth, shark, wolf, crocodile, ass, flea.
What germs, what jostling mobs there were in me.

  These seem like bristles, and the hide is tough.
No claw or web here: each foot ends in hoof.

Into what bulk has method disappeared?
Like ham, streaked. I am gross – grey, gross, flap-eared.

The pale-lashed eyes my only human feature.
My teeth tear, tear. I am the snouted creature

That bites through anything, root, wire, or can.
If I was not afraid I'd eat a man.

Oh a man's flesh already is in mine.
Hand and foot poised for risk. Buried in swine.

  I root and root, you think that it is greed,
It is, but I seek out a plant I need.

Direct me gods, whose changes are all holy,
To where it flickers deep in grass, the moly:

Cool flesh of magic in each leaf and shoot,
From milky flower to the black forked root.

From this fat dungeon I could rise to skin
And human title, putting pig within.

I push my big grey wet snout through the green,
Dreaming the flower I have never seen.

For Signs

1

In front of me, the palings of a fence
Throw shadows hard as board across the weeds;
The cracked enamel of a chicken bowl
Gleams like another moon; each clump of reeds
Is split with darkness and yet bristles whole.
The field survives, but with a difference.

And sleep like moonlight drifts and clings to shape.
My mind, which learns its freedom every day,
Sinks into vacancy but cannot rest.
While moonlight floods the pillow where it lay,
It walks among the past, weeping, obsessed,
Trying to master it and learn escape.

I dream: the real is shattered and combined,
Until the moon comes back into that sign
It stood in at my birth-hour; and I pass
Back to the field where, statued in the shine,
Someone is gazing upward from the grass
As if toward vaults that honeycomb the mind.

Slight figure in a wide black hat, whose hair
Massed and moon-coloured almost hides his face.
The thin white lips are dry, the eyes intense
Watching not thing, but lunar orgy, chase,
Trap, and cool fantasy of violence.
I recognize the pale long inward stare.

His tight young flesh is only on the top.
Beneath it, is an answering moon, at full,
Pitted with craters and with empty seas.
Dream mentor, I have been inside that skull,
I too have used those cindered passages.

But now the moon leaves Scorpio: I look up.

3

No, not inconstant, though it is called so.
For I have always found it waiting there,
Whether reduced to an invisible seed,
Or whether swollen again above the air
To rake the oubliettes of pain and greed
Opened at night in fellowship below.

It goes, and in its going it returns,
Cycle that I in part am governed by
And cannot understand where it is dark.
I lean upon the fence and watch the sky,
How light fills blinded socket and chafed mark.
It soars, hard, full, and edged, it coldly burns.

Three

All three are bare.
The father towels himself by two grey boulders
  Long body, then long hair,
Matted like rainy bracken, to his shoulders.

  The pull and risk
Of the Pacific's touch is yet with him:
  He kicked and felt it brisk,
Its cold live sinews tugging at each limb.

  It haunts him still:
Drying his loins, he grins to notice how,
  Struck helpless with the chill,
His cock hangs tiny and withdrawn there now.

  Near, eyes half-closed,
The mother lies back on the hot round stones,
  Her weight to theirs opposed
And pressing them as if they were earth's bones.

  Hard bone, firm skin,
She holds her breasts and belly up, now dry,
  Striped white where clothes have been,
To the heat that sponsors all heat, from the sky.

  Only their son
Is brown all over. Rapt in endless play,
  In which all games make one,
His three-year nakedness is everyday.

Swims as dogs swim.
Rushes his father, wriggles from his hold.
His body which is him,
Sturdy and volatile, runs off the cold.

Runs up to me:
Hi there hi there, he shrills, yet will not stop,
For though continually
Accepting everything his play turns up

He still leaves it
And comes back to that pebble-warmed recess
In which the parents sit,
At watch, who had to learn their nakedness.

From the Wave

It mounts at sea, a concave wall
    Down-ribbed with shine,
And pushes forward, building tall
    Its steep incline.

Then from their hiding rise to sight
    Black shapes on boards
Bearing before the fringe of white
    It mottles towards.

Their pale feet curl, they poise their weight
    With a learn'd skill.
It is the wave they imitate
    Keeps them so still.

The marbling bodies have become
    Half wave, half men,
Grafted it seems by feet of foam
    Some seconds, then,

Late as they can, they slice the face
    In timed procession:
Balance is triumph in this place,
    Triumph possession.

The mindless heave of which they rode
    A fluid shelf
Breaks as they leave it, falls and, slowed,
    Loses itself.

Clear, the sheathed bodies slick as seals
    Loosen and tingle;
And by the board the bare foot feels
    The suck of shingle.

They paddle in the shallows still;
    Two splash each other;
Then all swim out to wait until
    The right waves gather.

Street Song

I am too young to grow a beard
But yes man it was me you heard
In dirty denim and dark glasses.
I look through everyone who passes
But ask him clear, I do not plead,
Keys lids acid and speed.

My grass is not oregano.
Some of it grew in Mexico.
You cannot guess the weed I hold,
Clara Green, Acapulco Gold,
Panama Red, you name it man,
Best on the street since I began.

My methedrine, my double-sun,
Will give you two lives in your one,
Five days of power before you crash.
At which time use these lumps of hash
– They burn so sweet, they smoke so smooth,
They make you sharper while they soothe.

Now here, the best I've got to show,
Made by a righteous cat I know.
Pure acid – it will scrape your brain,
And make it something else again.
Call it heaven, call it hell,
Join me and see the world I sell.

Join me, and I will take you there,
Your head will cut out from your hair
Into whichever self you choose.
With Midday Mick man you can't lose,
I'll get you anything you need.
Keys lids acid and speed.

Grasses

Laurel and eucalyptus, dry sharp smells,
Pause in the dust of summer. But we sit
High on a fort, above grey blocks and wells,
And watch the restless grasses lapping it.

Each dulling-green, keen, streaky blade of grass
Leans to one body when the breezes start:
A one-time pathway flickers as they pass,
Where paler toward the root the quick ranks part.

The grasses quiver, rising from below.
I wait on warm rough concrete, I have time.
They round off all the lower steps, and blow
Like lights on bended water as they climb.

From some dark passage in the abandoned fort,
I hear a friend's harmonica – withdrawn sound,
A long whine drawling after several short . . .
The spiky body mounting from the ground.

A wail uneven all the afternoon,
Thin, slow, no noise of tramping nor of dance.
It is the sound, half tuneless and half tune,
With which the scattered details make advance.

Kirby's Cove

The Discovery of the Pacific

They lean against the cooling car, backs pressed
Upon the dust of a brown continent,
And watch the sun, now Westward of their West,
Fall to the ocean. Where it led they went.

Kansas to California. Day by day
They travelled emptier of the things they knew.
They improvised new habits on the way,
But lost the occasions, and then lost them too.

One night, no one and nowhere, she had woken
To resin-smell and to the firs' slight sound,
And through their sleeping-bag had felt the broken
Tight-knotted surfaces of the naked ground.

Only his lean quiet body cupping hers
Kept her from it, the extreme chill. By degrees
She fell asleep. Around them in the firs
The wind probed, tiding through forked estuaries.

And now their skin is caked with road, the grime
Merely reflecting sunlight as it fails.
They leave their clothes among the rocks they climb,
Blunt leaves of iceplant nuzzle at their soles.

Now they stand chin-deep in the sway of ocean,
Firm West, two stringy bodies face to face,
And come, together, in the water's motion,
The full caught pause of their embrace.

Sunlight

Some things, by their affinity light's token,
Are more than shown: steel glitters from a track;
Small glinting scoops, after a wave has broken,
Dimple the water in its draining back;

Water, glass, metal, match light in their raptures,
Flashing their many answers to the one.
What captures light belongs to what it captures:
The whole side of a world facing the sun,

Re-turned to woo the original perfection,
Giving itself to what created it,
And wearing green in sign of its subjection.
It is as if the sun were infinite.

But angry flaws are swallowed by the distance;
It varies, moves, its concentrated fires
Are slowly dying – the image of persistence
Is an image, only, of our own desires:

Desires and knowledge touch without relating.
The system of which sun and we are part
Is both imperfect and deteriorating.
And yet the sun outlasts us at the heart.

Great seedbed, yellow centre of the flower,
Flower on its own, without a root or stem,
Giving all colour and all shape their power,
Still recreating in defining them,

Enable us, altering like you, to enter
Your passionless love, impartial but intense,
And kindle in acceptance round your centre,
Petals of light lost in your innocence.

from
JACK STRAW'S CASTLE
(1976)

Diagrams

Downtown, an office tower is going up.
And from the mesa of unfinished top
Big cranes jut, spectral points of stiffened net:
Angled top-heavy artefacts, and yet
Diagrams from the sky, as if its air
Could drop lines, snip them off, and leave them there.

On girders round them, Indians pad like cats,
With wrenches in their pockets and hard hats.

They wear their yellow boots like moccasins,
Balanced where air ends and where steel begins,
Sky men, and through the sole's flesh, chewed and pliant,
They feel the studded bone-edge of the giant.
It grunts and sways through its whole metal length.
And giving to the air is sign of strength.

Iron Landscapes
(and the Statue of Liberty)

No trellises, no vines
                    a fire escape
Repeats a bare black Z from tier to tier.
Hard flower, tin scroll embellish this landscape.
Between iron columns I walk toward the pier.

And stand a long time at the end of it
Gazing at iron on the New Jersey side.
A girdered ferry-building opposite,
Displaying the name LACKAWANNA, seems to ride

The turbulent brown-grey waters that intervene:
Cool seething incompletion that I love.
The zigzags come and go, sheen tracking sheen;
And water wrestles with the air above.

But I'm at peace with the iron landscape too,
Hard because buildings must be hard to last
– Block, cylinder, cube, built with their angles true,
A dream of righteous permanence, from the past.

In Nixon's era, decades after the ferry,
The copper embodiment of the pieties
Seems hard, but hard like a revolutionary
With indignation, constant as she is.

From here you can glimpse her downstream, her far charm,
Liberty, tiny woman in the mist
– You cannot see the torch – raising her arm
Lorn, bold, as if saluting with her fist.

Morton Street Pier, New York, May 1973

Last Days at Teddington

The windows wide through day and night
Gave on the garden like a room.
The garden smell, green composite,
Flowed in and out a house in bloom.

To the shaggy dog who skidded from
The concrete through the kitchen door
To yellow-squared linoleum,
It was an undivided floor.

How green it was indoors. The thin
Pale creepers climbed up brick until
We saw their rolled tongues flicker in
Across the cracked paint of the sill.

How sociable the garden was.
We ate and talked in given light.
The children put their toys to grass
All the warm wakeful August night.

So coming back from drinking late
We picked our way below the wall
But in the higher grass, dewed wet,
Stumbled on tricycle and ball.

When everything was moved away,
The house returned to board and shelf,
And smelt of hot dust through the day,
The garden fell back on itself.

Jack Straw's Castle

I

Jack Straw sits
           sits in his castle
Jack Straw watches the rain

why can't I leave my castle
he says, isn't there anyone
anyone here besides me

sometimes I find myself wondering
if the castle is castle at all
a place apart, or merely
the castle that every snail
must carry around till his death

and then there's the matter of breath
on a cold day it rears before me
like a beautiful fern
I'm amazed at the plant

will it survive me
a man of no account
visited only by visions

and no one here
no one who knows how to play

visions, voices, burning smells
all of a rainy day

2

Pig Pig she cries
I can hear her from next door
He fucked me in the mouth
and now he won't give me car fare
she rages and cries

3

The rain stops. I look round: a square of floor,
Blond wood, shines palely in the laggard sun;
The kittens suck, contrasting strips of fur,
The mother in their box, a perfect fit;
I finally got it how I wanted it,
A fine snug house when all is said and done.

But night makes me uneasy: floor by floor
Rooms never guessed at open from the gloom
First as thin smoky lines, ghost of a door
Or lintel that develops like a print
Darkening into full embodiment
– Boudoir and oubliette, room on room on room.

And I have met or I believed I met
People in some of them, though they were not
The kind I need. They looked convincing, yet
There always was too much of the phantom to them.
Meanwhile, and even when I walked right through them,
I was talking, talking to myself. Of what?

Fact was, the echo of each word drowned out
The next word spoken, and I cannot say
What it was I was going on about.
It could be I was asking, Do these rooms
Spring up at night-time suddenly, like mushrooms,
Or have they all been hiding here all day?

4

Dream sponsors:
Charles Manson, tongue
playing over dry lips,
thinking a long thought;
and the Furies, mad
puppety heads appearing
in the open transom above
a forming door, like heads
of kittens staring angrily
over the edge of their box:

'Quick, fetch Medusa,'
their shrewish voices,
'Show him Medusa.'

Maybe I won't turn away,
maybe I'm so cool
I could outstare her.

5
The door opens.
There are no snakes.
The head
is on the table.

On the table
gold hair struck
by light from
the naked bulb,
a dazzle in which
the ground of dazzle
is consumed, the
hair burning
in its own gold.

And her eyes
gaze at me,
pale blue, but
blank as the eyes
of zombie or angel,
with the stunned
lack of expression
of one
who has beheld
the source of everything
and found it
the same as nothing.

In her dazzle I
catch fire
self-delighting
self-sufficient
self-consuming
till
I burn out
so heavy
I sink into
darkness into
my foundations.

6

Down in the cellars, nothing is visible
                              no one
Though there's a sound about me of many breathing
Light slap of foot on stone and rustle of body
Against body and stone.
                    And when later
I finger a stickiness along the ridges
Of a large central block that feels like granite
I don't know if it's my own, or I shed it,
Or both, as if priest and victim were only
Two limbs of the same body.
                              The lost traveller.
For this is the seat of needs
                    so deep, so old
That even where eye never perceives body
And where the sharpest ear discerns only

The light slap and rustle of flesh on stone
They, the needs, seek ritual and ceremony
To appease themselves
                              (Oh, the breathing all around me)
Or they would tear apart the life that feeds them.

                              7

I am the man on the rack.
I am the man who puts the man on the rack.
I am the man who watches the man who puts the man on the
    rack.

                              8
                    Might it not have been
                    a thought-up film
                    which suddenly ceases

                    the lights go up
                    I can see only
                    this pearl-grey chamber
                    false and quiet
                    no audience here
                    just the throned one

                    nothing outside the bone
                    nothing accessible

the ambush and taking of
meaning were nothing
                                    were
inventions of Little Ease

I sit
trapped in bone
I am back again
where I never left, I sit
in my first instant, where
I never left

petrified at my centre

                         9
I spin like a solitary star, I swoon.

But there breaks into my long solitude

A bearded face, it's Charlie, close as close,
His breath that stinks of jail – of pain and fungus,
So close that I breathe nothing else.

Then I recall as if it were my own
Life on the hot ranch, and the other smells.
Of laurel in the sun, fierce, sweet; of people
– Death-sweat or lust-sweat they smelt much the same.
He reigned in sultry power over his dream.

I come back to the face pushed into mine.
Tells me he's bound to point out, man,
That dreams don't come from nowhere: it's your dream
He says, you dreamt it. So there's no escape.

And now he's squatting at a distance
To wait the taunt's effect, paring his nails,
From time to time glancing up sideways at me,
A sly mad look. Yes, but he's not mad either.

He's gone too far, Charlie you've overdone it.
Something inside my head turns over.
I think I see how his taunt can be my staircase,
For if I brought all of this stuff inside
There must be an outside to bring it from.
Outside the castle, somewhere, there must be
A real Charles Manson, a real woman crying,
And laws I had no hand in, like gravity.

About midnight. Where earlier there had seemed
A shadowy arch projected on the bone-like stone,
I notice, fixing itself,
Easing itself in place even as I see it,
A staircase leading upward.
                                        Is that rain
Far overhead, that drumming sound?
Boy, what a climb ahead.

At the bottom, looking back, I find
He is, for now at any rate, clean gone.

10

My coldness wakes me,
mine, and the kitchen chair's.

How long have I sat here? I
went to sleep in bed.

Entering real rooms perhaps,
my own spectre, cold,

unshivering as a flight of
flint steps that leads nowhere,

in a ruin, where the wall
abruptly ends, and the steps too

and you stare down at the broken
slabs far below, at the ivy

glinting over bone-chips which must
at one time have been castle.

II

Down panic, down. The castle is still here,
And I am in the kitchen with a beer
Hearing the hurricane thin out to rain.
Got to relax if I'm to sleep again.
The castle is here, but not snug any more,
I'm loose, I rattle in its hollow core.
And as for that parade of rooms – shed, jail,
Cellar, each snapping at the next one's tail –
That raced inside my skull for half the night,
I hope I'm through with that. I flick the light.
And though the dungeon will be there for good
(What laid those stones?) at least I found I could,
Thrown down, escape by learning what to learn;
And hold it that held me.
                                        Till I return.

And so to bed, in hopes that I won't dream.

                        ..   ..   ..

I drift, doze, sleep. But toward dawn it does seem,
While I half-wake, too tired to turn my head,
That someone stirs behind me in the bed
Between two windows on an upper floor.
Is it a real man muttering? I'm not sure.
Though he does not seem phantom-like as yet,
Thick, heavily breathing, with a sweet faint sweat.

So humid, we lie sheetless – bare and close,
Facing apart, but leaning ass to ass.
And that mere contact is sufficient touch,
A hinge, it separates but not too much.
An air moves over us, as calm and cool
As the green water of a swimming pool.

What if this is the man I gave my key
Who got in while I slept? Or what if he,
Still, is a dream of that same man?
                                        No, real.
Comes from outside the castle, I can feel.
The beauty's in what is, not what may seem.
I turn. And even if he were a dream
– Thick sweating flesh against which I lie curled –
With dreams like this, Jack's ready for the world.

1973–4

An Amorous Debate

Leather Kid and Fleshly

Birds whistled, all
Nature was doing something while
Leather Kid and Fleshly
lay on a bank and
gleamingly discoursed
                        like this:
'You are so strong,' she said, 'such
a firm defence of hide against
the ripple of skin, it
excites me, all those
reserves suggested, though I do hope
that isn't a prosthetic device
under your glove is it?'

'Let's fuck,' he said.

She snuggled close, zipping
him open, unbuckling away
till he lay before her
                        a very
Mars unhorsed but
not doing much of
anything without his horse.

'Strange,' she said, 'you
are still encased in your
defence. You have
a hard cock but there is
something like the
obduracy of leather
still in your countenance
and your skin, it is like
a hide under hide.'
Then she laid the fierce
pale river of her body
against his, squashing
her lily breasts against
his hard male nipples, inserting
her thighs between his till
he fired a bit and
embracing her with some feeling
moved his head to suck at
the nearest flesh to
his mouth which turned out
to be his own arm.

Then a tremor passed
through his body, the sheen
fell from him, he
became wholly sensitive
as if his body had
rolled back its own foreskin.
(He began to sweat.)

And they melted one
into the other
            forthwith
like the way the Saône
joins the Rhône at Lyon.

Autobiography

The sniff of the real, that's
what I'd want to get
            how it felt
to sit on Parliament
Hill on a May evening
studying for exams   skinny
seventeen   dissatisfied
            yet sniffing such
a potent air, smell of
grass in heat from
the day's sun

I'd been walking through the damp
rich ways by the ponds
and now lay on the upper
grass with Lamartine's poems

life seemed all
loss, and what was more
I'd lost whatever it was
before I'd even had it

a green dry prospect
distant babble of children
and beyond, distinct at
the end of the glow
St Paul's like a stone thimble

longing so hard to make
inclusions that the longing
has become   in memory
an inclusion

Yoko

All today I lie in the bottom of the wardrobe
feeling low but sometimes getting up
to moodily lumber across rooms
and lap from the toilet bowl, it is so sultry
and then I hear the noise of firecrackers again
all New York is jaggedy with firecrackers today
and I go back to the wardrobe gloomy
trying to void my mind of them.
I am confused, I feel loose and unfitted.

At last deep in the stairwell I hear a tread,
it is him, my leader, my love.
I run to the door and listen to his approach.
Now I can smell him, what a good man he is,
I love it when he has the sweat of work on him,
as he enters I yodel with happiness,
I throw my body up against his, I try to lick his lips,
I care about him more than anything.

After we eat we go for a walk to the piers.
I leap into the standing warmth, I plunge into
the combination of old and new smells.
Here on a garbage can at the bottom, so interesting,
what sister or brother I wonder left this message I sniff.
I too piss there, and go on.
Here a hydrant there a pole
here's a smell I left yesterday, well that's disappointing
but I piss there anyway, and go on.

I investigate so much that in the end
it is for form's sake only, only a drop comes out.

I investigate tar and rotten sandwiches, everything, and go on.

And here a dried old turd, so interesting
so old, so dry, yet so subtle and mellow.
I can place it finely, I really appreciate it,
a gold distant smell like packed autumn leaves in winter
reminding me how what is rich and fierce when excreted
becomes weathered and mild
                              but always interesting
and reminding me of what I have to do.

My leader looks on and expresses his approval.

I sniff it well and later I sniff the air well
a wind is meeting us after the close July day
rain is getting near too but first the wind.

Joy, joy,
being outside with you, active, investigating it all,
with bowels emptied, feeling your approval
and then running on, the big fleet Yoko,
my body in its excellent black coat never lets me down,

returning to you (as I always will, you know that)
and now
        filling myself out with myself, no longer confused,
my panting pushing apart my black lips, but unmoving,
I stand with you braced against the wind.

from
THE PASSAGES OF JOY
(1982)

Expression

For several weeks I have been reading
the poetry of my juniors.
Mother doesn't understand,
and they hate Daddy, the noted alcoholic.
They write with black irony
of breakdown, mental institution,
and suicide attempt, of which the experience
does not always seem first-hand.
It is very poetic poetry.

I go to the Art Museum
and find myself looking for something,
though I'm not sure what it is.
I reach it, I recognize it,
seeing it for the first time.
An 'early Italian altar piece'.
The outlined Virgin, her lips
a strangely modern bow of red,
holds a doll-sized Child in her lap.
He has the knowing face of an adult,
and a precocious forelock curling
over the smooth baby forehead. She
is massive and almost symmetrical.
He does not wriggle, nor is he solemn.
The sight quenches, like water
after too much birthday cake.
Solidly there, mother and child
stare outward, two pairs of matching eyes
void of expression.

Sweet Things

He licks the last chocolate ice cream
from the scabbed corners of his mouth.
Sitting in the sun on a step
outside the laundromat,
mongoloid Don turns his crewcut head
and spies me coming down the street.
'Hi!' He says it with the mannered
enthusiasm of a fraternity brother.
'Take me cross the street!?' part
question part command. I hold
the sticky bunch of small fingers in mine
and we stumble across. They sell
peaches and pears over there,
the juice will dribble down your chin.
He turns before I leave him,
saying abruptly with the same
mixture of order and request
'Gimme a quarter!?' I
don't give it, never have, not to him,
I wonder why not, and as I
walk on alone I realize
it's because his unripened mind
never recognizes me, me
for myself, he only says hi
for what he can get, quarters to
buy sweet things, one after another,
he goes from store to store, from
candy store to ice cream store to
bakery to produce market, unending

quest for the palate's pleasure. Then
out to panhandle again,
more quarters, more sweet things.

My errands are toothpaste,
vitamin pills and a book of stamps.
No self-indulgence there.
But who's this coming up? It's
John, no Chuck, how
could his name have slipped my mind.
Chuck gives a one-sided smile, he stands
as if fresh from a laundromat,
a scrubbed cowboy, Tom Sawyer
grown up, yet stylish, perhaps
even careful, his dark hair
slicked back in the latest manner.
When he shakes my hand I feel
a dry finger playfully bending inward
and touching my palm in secret.
'It's a long time
since we got together,' says John.
Chuck, that is. The warm teasing
tickle in the cave of our handshake
took my mind off toothpaste,
snatched it off, indeed.
How handsome he is in
his lust and energy, in his
fine display of impulse.
Boldly 'How about now?' I say

knowing the answer. My boy
I could eat you whole. In the long pause
I gaze at him up and down and
from his blue sneakers back to the redawning
one-sided smile. We know our charm.
We know delay makes pleasure great.
In our eyes, on our tongues,
we savour the approaching delight
of things we know yet are fresh always.
Sweet things. Sweet things.

June

In these two separate rooms we sit,
I at my work, you at yours.
I am at once buried in it
And sensible of all outdoors.

The month is cool, as if on guard,
High fog holds back the sky for days,
But in their sullen patch of yard
The Oriental Poppies blaze.

Separate in the same weather
The parcelled buds crack pink and red,
And rise from different plants together
To shed their bud-sheaths on the bed,

And stretch their crumpled petals free,
That nurse the box of hardening seed,
In the same hour, as if to agree
On what could not have been agreed.

San Francisco Streets

I've had my eye on you
    For some time now.
You're getting by it seems,
    Not quite sure how.
But as you go along
    You're finding out
What different city streets
    Are all about.

Peach country was your home.
    When you went picking
You ended every day
    With peach fuzz sticking
All over face and arms,
    Intimate, gross,
Itching like family,
    And far too close.

But when you came to town
    And when you first
Hung out on Market Street
    That was the worst:
Tough little group of boys
    Outside Flagg's Shoes.
You learned to keep your cash.
    You got tattoos.

Then by degrees you rose
    Like country cream –
Hustler to towel boy,
    Bath house and steam;
Tried being kept a while –
    But felt confined,
One brass bed driving you
    Out of your mind.

Later on Castro Street
    You got new work
Selling chic jewelry.
    And as sales clerk
You have at last attained
    To middle class.
(No one on Castro Street
    Peddles his ass.)

You gaze out from the store.
    Watching you watch
All the men strolling by
    I think I catch
Half-veiled uncertainty
    In your expression.
Good looks and great physiques
    Pass in procession.

You've risen up this high –
    How, you're not sure.
Better remember what
    Makes you secure.
Fuzz is still on the peach,
    Peach on the stem.
Your looks looked after you.
    Look after them.

Transients and Residents

a sequence interrupted

'Albert Hotel,
    Transients and Residents'
        – NEW YORK, 1970

'Time hovers o'er, impatient to destroy,
And shuts up all the Passages of Joy.'
    SAMUEL JOHNSON
    'THE VANITY OF HUMAN WISHES'

Falstaff

I always hope to find you circling here
Round the bar's table, playing your old game,
In one hand pool cue, in the other beer.
Vast in your foul burnoose, you'd be the same:
Bullying your little entourage of boys
– Goodlooking but untrustworthy – and later
Ordering them home where, turning up the noise,
You'd party through the night. Neighbourhood satyr,
Old friend, for years you bullied all of us
And did so, you were sure, for our own good.
You took no notice if we made a fuss
Or didn't enjoy ourselves the way we should.
I think of one place you were living at
And all the parties that you used to throw
(That must be when you wore a feathered hat,
Several burnooses, so to speak, ago);
You cooked each evening for some twenty heads,
Not just for streetboys then, for everyone

Who came in want of food or drugs or beds.
The bonus was your boisterous sense of fun.
And though as years have passed your bullying love
Became more desperate (sometimes indeed
Stripped by a ruthlessness you weren't above
It showed itself more nakedly as need);
And though the parties that you gave took place
In other people's houses now, until
They kicked you out for taking all the space;
And though the drugs themselves got questionable –
Too many evenings in the bar have passed
Full of mere chatter and the pumping sound
Of disco on the juke box since you last
Roared down it for next player or next round.

If you are sick – that's what they say in here
Almost as if by way of an excuse –
The cancer must have rendered you, my dear.
Damnably thin beneath the foul burnoose.

Crystal

He arrives, and makes deliveries, after 3:00,
Then strolls to a ramp that leads up from the dance,
And sits apart, quiet, hands clasped round a knee,
Smelling the fresh-sawed planks, no doubt. Not tense –
Fixed, merely. While he watches us, his face
Is almost readable, his recessed shape
Gleams like a friendly visitor's from space.

As in a sense it is, now. To escape
The sheer impurity of the other lives,
He has always been extreme, he puts his soul
Into each role in turn, where he survives
Till it is incarnation more than role.
Now it is Dealer. 52, tall, scarred,
His looks get nobler every year, I find,
Almost heroic.
                        I once saw in the yard
A half-grown foxglove that he brings to mind
Here, so magnificently self-enwrapped.
Its outer leaves were toothed and all alike.
With a rough symmetry they overlapped
Circling around the budded central spike,
Still green. Dense with its destiny, it waited
Till it might fling itself up into flower.

Now he sits similarly concentrated,
And edged, and similarly charged with power,
Certain of that potential, which his mood
Fairly feeds on, but which is still contained.

The foxglove flowers in its damp solitude
Before its energy fades, and in the end
The chemical in the man will fade as well.
Meanwhile he watches how the dancing feet
Move to the rhythms of the fresh wood-smell;
Inside the crowded night he feels complete.

Crosswords

Your cup of instant coffee by the bed
Cold as the Sixties . . . and you chat with me.
For days your excellent strict mind has fed
Only on crossword puzzles and TV.
Though the least self-indulgent man I know
You lie propped up here like an invalid
Pursuing your recuperation, slow,
Relentless, from the world you used to need.
You have seen reason to remove your ground
Far from the great circle where you toiled,
Where they still call their wares and mill around
Body to body, unpausing and unspoiled.
You smell of last week. You do not move much.
You lay your things beside you on the bed
In a precarious pile one sudden touch
Would bring down on you: letters read and reread,
Pens, opera programmes, cigarettes and books.
I think you disturb nothing but the mind.
There: I catch one of those familiar looks
Of thinking through. You reach, you almost find.
Beneath a half-frown your eyes concentrate,
Focused on what you saw or dreamt you saw,
Alight with their attentiveness, and wait.
Yes, you are active still, you can't withdraw.

Now we take up again the much-discussed
The never-settled topics, (a) change, (b)
Limits of judgment, and of course (c) trust.
We talk, explore, agree and disagree.
   . . . I think that you just put me in the wrong.

You want to win, old jesuit. So do I.
You never liked it easy for too long.
I once found that this bed on which you lie
Is just a blanket-covered length of board.
For you, hardness authenticates, and when
Things get too easy, well you make them hard.
. . . We compromise. Then off we go again,
On our renewed cross-country walking tour,
Off with a swinging stride uphill. Stop, though,
Before there's time to disagree once more.
I want to tell you what you no doubt know:
How glad I am to be back at your school
Where it's through contradictions that I learn.
Obsessive and detached, ardent and cool,
You make me think of rock thrown free to turn
At the globe's side, both with and not with us,
Keeping yourself in a companionable
Chilled orbit by the simultaneous
Repulsion and attraction to it all.

Interruption

Though ready in my chair I do not write.
The desk lamp crook'd above me where I lean
Describes a circle round me with its light
– Singling me out; the room falls back unseen.
So, my own island. I can hear the rain
Coming on stealthily, and the rustle grows
Into a thin taptapping on the pane
I stare against, where my reflection glows.

Beyond by day shows that damp square of earth
On which I act out my experiments
– Sowing a seed and watching for the birth:
A tiny pair of leaves, pale rudiments
That might in time grow stronger to assume
A species' characteristics, till I see
Each fresh division soaring into bloom,
Beauty untouched by personality.

My mind shifts inward from such images.
What am I after – and what makes me think
The group of poems I have entered is
Interconnected by a closer link
Than any snapshot album's?
                                        I can try
At least to get my snapshots accurate.
(The thought that I take others' pictures, I,
Far too conceited to find adequate
Pictures they take of me!) Starting outside,
You save yourself some time while working in:
Thus by the seen the unseen is implied.

I like loud music, bars, and boisterous men.
You may from this conclude I like the things
That help me if not lose then leave behind,
What else, the self.
                    I trust the seedling wings,
Yet taking off on them I leave to find.

I find what? In the letters that I send
I imitate unconsciously the style
Of the recipients: mimicking each friend,
I answer expectations, and meanwhile
Can analyse, or drawl a page of wit,
And range, depending on the friend addressed,
From literary to barely literate.
I manage my mere voice on postcards best.

My garden is the plants that I have got
By luck, skill, purchase, robbery, or gift.
From foxglove, lily, pink, and bergamot
I raise leafed unity, a blossoming drift
Where I once found weed waiting out a drought.
But this side of the glass, dry as at noon,
I see the features that my lamp picks out –
Colourless, unjoined, like a damaged moon.

Talbot Road

(where I lived in London 1964–5)

in memory of Tony White

I

Between the pastel boutiques
of Notting Hill and the less defined
windier reaches of the Harrow Road,
all blackened brick, was the street
built for burghers, another Belgravia,
but eventually fallen
to labourers ('No Coloured or Irish
Need Apply') and then like the veins
of the true-born Englishman
filling with a promiscuous mix:
Pole, Italian, Irish, Jamaican,
rich jostling flow. A Yugoslav restaurant
framed photographs of exiled princes,
but the children chattered with a London accent.
I lived on Talbot Road
for a year. The excellent room
where I slept, ate, read, and wrote,
had a high ceiling, on the borders
stucco roses were painted blue.
You could step through the window
to a heavy balcony and even
(unless the drain was blocked)
sup there on hot evenings.
That's what I call complete access –

to air, to street, to friendship:
for, from it, I could see, blocks away,
the window where Tony, my old friend,
toiled at translation. I too tried
to render obscure passages into clear English,
as I try now.

2

Glamorous and difficult friend,
helper and ally. As students
enwrapt by our own romanticism,
innocent poet and actor we had posed
we had played out parts to each other
I have sometimes thought
like studs in a whorehouse.
– But he had to deal
with the best looks of his year.
If 'the rich are different from us',
so are the handsome. What
did he really want? Ah that question . . .

Two romances going on in London,
one in Northampton, one in Ireland,
probably others. Friends and lovers
all had their own versions of him.
Fantastical duke of dark corners,
he never needed to lie:
you had learned not to ask questions.

The fire of his good looks.
But almost concealed by the fringe of fire,
behind the mighty giving of self,
at the centre of the jollity, there was
something withheld, slow, something –
what? what? A damp smoulder of discontent.
He would speculate about 'human relations'
which we were supposed to view
– *vide* Forster, *passim*, etc. –
as an end, a good in themselves.
He did not find them so.

Finally it came to this,
the poses had come undone so far:
he loved you more for your faults
than for anything you could give him.
When once in a pub I lost my temper,
I shouldered my way back from the urinal
and snapped, 'I was too angry to piss.'
The next day he exclaimed with delight,
'Do you know that was the first time
you have ever been angry with me?'
As some people wait for a sign of love,
he had waited how many years
for a sign of anger,
for a sign of other than love.

3

A London returned to after twelve years.
On a long passage between two streets
I met my past self lingering there
or so he seemed
a youth of about nineteen glaring at me
from a turn of desire. He held his look
as if shielding it from wind.
Our eyes parleyed, then we touched
in the conversation of bodies.
Standing together on asphalt openly,
we gradually loosened into a shared laughter.
This was the year, the year of reconciliation
to whatever it was I had come from,
the prickly heat of adolescent emotion,
premature staleness and self-contempt.
In my hilarity, in my luck,
I forgave myself for having had a youth.

I started to heap up pardons
even in anticipation. On Hampstead Heath
I knew every sudden path from childhood,
the crooks of every climbable tree.
And now I engaged these at night,
and where I had played hide and seek
with neighbour children, played as an adult
with troops of men whose rounds intersected
at the Orgy Tree or in the wood

of birch trunks gleaming like mute watchers
or in tents of branch and bush
surrounded by the familiar smell
of young leaf – salty, explosive.
In a Forest of Arden, in a summer night's dream
I forgave everybody his teens.

4

But I came back, after the last bus,
from Hampstead, Wimbledon, the pubs,
the railway arches of the East End,
I came back to Talbot Road,
to the brick, the cement Arthurian faces,
the area railings by coal holes,
the fat pillars of the entrances.
My balcony filled up with wet snow.
When it dried out Tony and I
would lunch there in the sunshine
on veal-and-ham pie, beer, and salad.
I told him about my adventures.
He wondered aloud if he would be happier
if he were queer like me.
How could he want, I wondered,
to be anything but himself?
Then he would have to be off,
off with his jaunty walk,
where, I didn't ask or guess.

At the end of my year, before I left,
he held a great party for me
on a canal boat. The party slipped
through the watery network of London,
grid that had always been glimpsed
out of the corner of the eye
behind fences or from the tops of buses.
Now here we were, buoyant on it,
picnicking, gazing in mid-mouthful
at the backs of buildings, at smoke-black walls
coral in the light of the long evening,
at what we had suspected all along
when we crossed the bridges we now passed under,
gliding through the open secret.

                        5
That was fifteen years ago.
Tony is dead, the block where I lived
has been torn down. The mind
is an impermanent place, isn't it,
but it looks to permanence.
The street has opened and opened up
into no character at all. Last night
I dreamt of it as it might have been,
the pavement by the church railings
was wet with spring rain,
it was night, the streetlamps' light

rendered it into an exquisite etching.
Sentimental postcard of a dream,
of a moment between race-riots!

But I do clearly remember my last week,
when every detail brightened with meaning.
A boy was staying with (I would think)
his grandmother in the house opposite.
He was in his teens, from the country perhaps.
Every evening of that week
he sat in his white shirt at the window
– a Gothic arch of reduced proportion –
leaning on his arms, gazing down
as if intently making out characters
from a live language he was still learning,
not a smile cracking his pink cheeks.
Gazing down
at the human traffic, of all nations,
the just and the unjust, who
were they, where were they going,
that fine public flow at the edge of which
he waited, poised, detached in wonder
and in no hurry
before he got ready one day
to climb down into its live current.

Night Taxi

for Rod Taylor
wherever he is

Open city
uncluttered as a map.
I drive through empty streets
scoured by the winds
of midnight. My shift
is only beginning and I am fresh
and excitable, master of the taxi.
I relish my alert reflexes
where all else
is in hiding. I have
by default it seems
conquered me a city.

My first address: I
press the doorbell, I lean back
against the hood, my headlights
scalding a garage door, my engine
drumming in the driveway,
the only sound on the block.
There the fare finds me
like a date, jaunty,
shoes shined, I am
proud of myself, on my toes,
obliging but not subservient.

I take short cuts, picking up
speed, from time to time
I switch on the dispatcher's
litany of addresses,
China Basin to Twin Peaks,
Harrison Street to the Ocean.

I am thinking tonight
my fares are like affairs
– no, more like tricks to turn:
quick, lively, ending up
with a cash payment.
I do not anticipate a holdup.
I can make friendly small talk.
I do not go on about Niggers,
women drivers or the Chinese.
It's all on my terms but
I let them think it's on theirs.

Do I pass through the city
or does it pass through me?
I know I have to be loose,
like my light embrace of the wheel,
loose but in control
– though hour by hour I tighten
minutely in the routine,
smoking my palate to ash,
till the last hour of all
will be drudgery, nothing else.

I zip down Masonic Avenue,
the taxi sings beneath the streetlights
a song to the bare city, it is
my instrument, I woo with it,
bridegroom and conqueror.

I jump out to open the door,
fixing the cap on my head
to, you know, firm up my role,
and on my knuckle
feel a sprinkle of wet.

Glancing upward I see
high above the lamppost
but touched by its farthest light
a curtain of rain already blowing
against black eucalyptus tops.

from
THE MAN WITH NIGHT SWEATS
(1992)

The Hug

It was your birthday, we had drunk and dined
   Half of the night with our old friend
     Who'd showed us in the end
   To a bed I reached in one drunk stride.
     Already I lay snug,
And drowsy with the wine dozed on one side.

I dozed, I slept. My sleep broke on a hug,
     Suddenly, from behind,
In which the full lengths of our bodies pressed:
     Your instep to my heel,
   My shoulder-blades against your chest.
   It was not sex, but I could feel
   The whole strength of your body set,
     Or braced, to mine,
     And locking me to you
   As if we were still twenty-two
   When our grand passion had not yet
     Become familial.
   My quick sleep had deleted all
   Of intervening time and place.
     I only knew
The stay of your secure firm dry embrace.

The Differences

Reciting Adrienne Rich on Cole and Haight,
Your blond hair bouncing like a corner boy's,
You walked with sturdy almost swaggering gait,
The short man's, looking upward with such poise,
Such bold yet friendly curiosity
I was convinced that clear defiant blue
Would have abashed a storm-trooper. To me
Conscience and courage stood fleshed out in you.

So when you gnawed my armpits, I gnawed yours
And learned to associate you with that smell
As if your exuberance sprang from your pores.
I tried to lose my self in you as well.
To lose my self . . . I did the opposite,
I turned into the boy with iron teeth
Who planned to eat the whole world bit by bit,
My love not flesh but in the mind beneath.

Love takes its shape within that part of me
(A poet says) *where memories reside.*
And just as light marks out the boundary
Of some glass outline men can see inside,
So love is formed by a dark ray's invasion
From Mars, its dwelling in the mind to make.
Is a created thing, and has sensation,
A soul, and strength of will.
                                    It is opaque.

Opaque, yet once I slept with you all night
Dreaming about you – though not quite embraced
Always in contact felt however slight.
We lay at ease, an arm loose round a waist,
Or side by side and touching at the hips,
As if we were two trees, bough grazing bough,
The twigs being the toes or fingertips.
I have not crossed your mind for three weeks now,

But think back on that night in January,
When casually distinct we shared the most
And lay upon a bed of clarity
In luminous half-sleep where the will was lost.
We woke at times and as the night got colder
Exchanged a word, or pulled the clothes again
To cover up the other's exposed shoulder,
Falling asleep to the small talk of the rain.

Skateboard

Tow Head on his skateboard
threads through a crowd
of feet and faces delayed
to a slow stupidity.
Darts, doubles, twists.
You notice how nimbly
the body itself has learned
to assess the relation between
the board, pedestrians,
and immediate sidewalk.
Emblem. Emblem of fashion.
Wearing dirty white
in dishevelment as delicate
as the falling draperies
on a dandyish
Renaissance saint.
Chain round his waist.
One hand gloved.
Hair dyed to show it is dyed,
pale flame spiking from fuel.
Tow Head on Skateboard
perfecting himself:
emblem extraordinary
of the ordinary.

In the sexless face
eyes innocent of feeling
therefore suggest the spirit.

To Isherwood Dying

It could be, Christopher, from your leafed-in house
In Santa Monica where you lie and wait
    You hear outside a sound resume
      Fitful, anonymous,
    Of Berlin fifty years ago
    As autumn days got late –
The whistling to their girls from young men who
    Stood in the deep dim street, below
Dingy façades which crumbled like a cliff,
    Behind which in a rented room
      You listened, wondering if
By chance one might be whistling up for you,
    Adding unsentimentally
      'It could not possibly be.'
Now it's a stricter vigil that you hold
And from the canyon's palms and crumbled gold
      It could be possibly
    You hear a single whistle call
      Come out
    Come out into the cold.
Courting insistent and impersonal.

Christmas week, 1985

The Stealer

I lie and live
my body's fear
something's at large
and coming near

No deadbolt
can keep it back
A worm of fog
leaks through a crack

From the darkness
as before
it grows to body
in my door

Like a taker
scarved and gloved
it steals this way
like one I loved

Fear stiffens me
and a slow joy
at the approach
of the sheathed boy

Will he too do
what that one did
unlock me first
open the lid

and reach inside
with playful feel
all the better
thus to steal

Nasturtium

Born in a sour waste lot
You laboured up to light,
Bunching what strength you'd got
And running out of sight
Through a knot-hole at last,
To come forth into sun
As if without a past,
Done with it, re-begun.

Now street-side of the fence
You take a few green turns,
Nimble in nonchalance
Before your first flower burns.
From poverty and prison
And undernourishment
A prodigal has risen,
Self-spending, never spent.

Irregular yellow shell
And drooping spur behind . . .
Not rare but beautiful
– Street-handsome – as you wind
And leap, hold after hold,
A golden runaway
Still running, strewing gold
From side to side all day.

The Man with Night Sweats

I wake up cold, I who
Prospered through dreams of heat
Wake to their residue,
Sweat, and a clinging sheet.

My flesh was its own shield:
Where it was gashed, it healed.

I grew as I explored
The body I could trust
Even while I adored
The risk that made robust,

A world of wonders in
Each challenge to the skin.

I cannot but be sorry
The given shield was cracked
My mind reduced to hurry,
My flesh reduced and wrecked.

I have to change the bed,
But catch myself instead

Stopped upright where I am
Hugging my body to me
As if to shield it from
The pains that will go through me,

As if hands were enough
To hold an avalanche off.

Lament

Your dying was a difficult enterprise.
First, petty things took up your energies,
The small but clustering duties of the sick,
Irritant as the cough's dry rhetoric.
Those hours of waiting for pills, shot, X-ray
Or test (while you read novels two a day)
Already with a kind of clumsy stealth
Distanced you from the habits of your health.
In hope still, courteous still, but tired and thin,
You tried to stay the man that you had been,
Treating each symptom as a mere mishap
Without import. But then the spinal tap.
It brought a hard headache, and when night came
I heard you wake up from the same bad dream
Every half-hour with the same short cry
Of mild outrage, before immediately
Slipping into the nightmare once again
Empty of content but the drip of pain.
No respite followed: though the nightmare ceased,
Your cough grew thick and rich, its strength increased.
Four nights, and on the fifth we drove you down
To the Emergency Room. That frown, that frown:
I'd never seen such rage in you before
As when they wheeled you through the swinging door.
For you knew, rightly, they conveyed you from
Those normal pleasures of the sun's kingdom
The hedonistic body basks within
And takes for granted – summer on the skin,
Sleep without break, the moderate taste of tea

In a dry mouth. You had gone on from me
As if your body sought out martyrdom
In the far Canada of a hospital room.
Once there, you entered fully the distress
And long pale rigours of the wilderness.
A gust of morphine hid you. Back in sight
You breathed through a segmented tube, fat, white,
Jammed down your throat so that you could not speak.
How thin the distance made you. In your cheek
One day, appeared the true shape of your bone
No longer padded. Still your mind, alone,
Explored this emptying intermediate
State for what holds and rests were hidden in it.
You wrote us messages on a pad, amused
At one time that you had your nurse confused
Who, seeing you reconciled after four years
With your grey father, both of you in tears,
Asked if this was at last your 'special friend'
(The one you waited for until the end).
'She sings,' you wrote, 'a Philippine folk song
To wake me in the morning . . . It is long
And very pretty.' Grabbing at detail
To furnish this bare ledge toured by the gale,
On which you lay, bed restful as a knife,
You tried, tried hard, to make of it a life
Thick with the complicating circumstance
Your thoughts might fasten on. It had been chance
Always till now that had filled up the moment
With live specifics your hilarious comment

Discovered as it went along; and fed,
Laconic, quick, wherever it was led.
You improvised upon your own delight.
I think back to the scented summer night
We talked between our sleeping bags, below
A molten field of stars five years ago:
I was so tickled by your mind's light touch
I couldn't sleep, you made me laugh too much,
Though I was tired and begged you to leave off.

Now you were tired, and yet not tired enough
– Still hungry for the great world you were losing
Steadily in no season of your choosing –
And when at last the whole death was assured,
Drugs having failed, and when you had endured
Two weeks of an abominable constraint,
You faced it equably, without complaint,
Unwhimpering, but not at peace with it.
You'd lived as if your time was infinite:
You were not ready and not reconciled,
Feeling as uncompleted as a child
Till you had shown the world what you could do
In some ambitious role to be worked through,
A role your need for it had half-defined,
But never wholly, even in your mind.
You lacked the necessary ruthlessness,
The soaring meanness that pinpoints success.
We loved that lack of self-love, and your smile,
Rueful, at your own silliness.

Meanwhile,
Your lungs collapsed, and the machine, unstrained,
Did all your breathing now. Nothing remained
But death by drowning on an inland sea
Of your own fluids, which it seemed could be
Kindly forestalled by drugs. Both could and would:
Nothing was said, everything understood,
At least by us. Your own concerns were not
Long-term, precisely, when they gave the shot
– You made local arrangements to the bed
And pulled a pillow round beside your head.
    And so you slept, and died, your skin gone grey,
Achieving your completeness, in a way.

Outdoors next day, I was dizzy from a sense
Of being ejected with some violence
From vigil in a white and distant spot
Where I was numb, into this garden plot
Too warm, too close, and not enough like pain.
I was delivered into time again
– The variations that I live among
Where your long body too used to belong
And where the still bush is minutely active.
You never thought your body was attractive,
Though others did, and yet you trusted it
And must have loved its fickleness a bit
Since it was yours and gave you what it could,
Till near the end it let you down for good,
Its blood hospitable to those guests who

Took over by betraying it into
The greatest of its inconsistencies
This difficult, tedious, painful enterprise.

Terminal

The eight years difference in age seems now
Disparity so wide between the two
That when I see the man who armoured stood
Resistant to all help however good
Now helped through day itself, eased into chairs,
Or else led step by step down the long stairs
With firm and gentle guidance by his friend,
Who loves him, through each effort to descend,
Each wavering, each attempt made to complete
An arc of movement and bring down the feet
As if with that spare strength he used to enjoy,
I think of Oedipus, old, led by a boy.

Her Pet

I walk the floor, read, watch a cop-show, drink,
Hear buses heave uphill through drizzling fog,
Then turn back to the pictured book to think
Of Valentine Balbiani and her dog:
She is reclining, reading, on her tomb;
But pounced, it tries to intercept her look,
Its front paws on her lap, as in this room
The cat attempts to nose beneath my book.

Her curls tight, breasts held by her bodice high,
Ruff crisp, mouth calm, hands long and delicate,
All in the pause of marble signify
A strength so lavish she can limit it.
She will not let her pet dog catch her eye
For dignity, and for a touch of wit.

Below, from the same tomb, is reproduced
A side-relief, in which she reappears
Without her dog, and everything is loosed –
Her hair down from the secret of her ears,
Her big ears, and her creased face genderless
Craning from sinewy throat. Death is so plain!
Her breasts are low knobs through the unbound dress.
In the worked features I can read the pain
She went through to get here, to shake it all,
Thinking at first that her full nimble strength
Hid like a little dog within recall,

Till to think so, she knew, was to pretend
And, hope dismissed, she sought out pain at length
And laboured with it to bring on its end.

The J Car

Last year I used to ride the J CHURCH Line,
Climbing between small yards recessed with vine
– Their ordered privacy, their plots of flowers
Like blameless lives we might imagine ours.
Most trees were cut back, but some brushed the car
Before it swung round to the street once more
On which I rolled out almost to the end,
To 29th Street, calling for my friend.
    He'd be there at the door, smiling but gaunt,
To set out for the German restaurant.
There, since his sight was tattered now, I would
First read the menu out. He liked the food
In which a sourness and dark richness meet
For conflict without taste of a defeat,
As in the Sauerbraten. What he ate
I hoped would help him to put on some weight,
But though the crusted pancakes might attract
They did so more as concept than in fact,
And I'd eat his dessert before we both
Rose from the neat arrangement of the cloth,
Where the connection between life and food
Had briefly seemed so obvious if so crude.
Our conversation circumspectly cheerful,
We had sat here like children good but fearful
Who think if they behave everything might
Still against likelihood come out all right.
    But it would not, and we could not stay here:
Finishing up the Optimator beer
I walked him home through the suburban cool

By dimming shape of church and Catholic school,
Only a few, white, teenagers about.
After the four blocks he would be tired out.
I'd leave him to the feverish sleep ahead,
Myself to ride through darkened yards instead
Back to my health. Of course I simplify.
Of course. It tears me still that he should die
As only an apprentice to his trade,
The ultimate engagements not yet made.
His gifts had been withdrawing one by one
Even before their usefulness was done:
This optic nerve would never be relit;
The other flickered, soon to be with it.
Unready, disappointed, unachieved,
He knew he would not write the much-conceived
Much-hoped-for work now, nor yet help create
A love he might in full reciprocate.

The Missing

Now as I watch the progress of the plague,
The friends surrounding me fall sick, grow thin,
And drop away. Bared, is my shape less vague
– Sharply exposed and with a sculpted skin?

I do not like the statue's chill contour,
Not nowadays. The warmth investing me
Led outward through mind, limb, feeling, and more
In an involved increasing family.

Contact of friend led to another friend,
Supple entwinement through the living mass
Which for all that I knew might have no end,
Image of an unlimited embrace.

I did not just feel ease, though comfortable:
Aggressive as in some ideal of sport,
With ceaseless movement thrilling through the whole,
Their push kept me as firm as their support.

But death – Their deaths have left me less defined:
It was their pulsing presence made me clear.
I borrowed from it, I was unconfined,
Who tonight balance unsupported here,

Eyes glaring from raw marble, in a pose
Languorously part-buried in the block,
Shins perfect and no calves, as if I froze
Between potential and a finished work.

– Abandoned incomplete, shape of a shape,
In which exact detail shows the more strange,
Trapped in unwholeness, I find no escape
Back to the play of constant give and change.

August 1987

from
BOSS CUPID
(2000)

Duncan

1

When in his twenties a poetry's full strength
Burst into voice as an unstopping flood,
He let the divine prompting (come at length)
Rushingly bear him any way it would
And went on writing while the Ferry turned
From San Francisco, back from Berkeley too,
And back again, and back again. He learned
You add to, you don't cancel what you do.

Between the notebook-margins his pen travelled,
His own lines carrying him in a new mode
To ports in which past purposes unravelled.
So that, as on the Ferry Line he rode,
Whatever his first plans that night had been,
The energy that rose from their confusion
Became the changing passage lived within
While the pen wrote, and looked beyond conclusion.

Forty years later, and both kidneys gone;
Every eight hours, home dialysis;
The habit of his restlessness stayed on
Exhausting him with his responsiveness.
After the circulations of one day
In which he taught a three-hour seminar
Then gave a reading clear across the Bay,
And while returning from it to the car

With plunging hovering tread tired and unsteady
Down Wheeler steps, he faltered and he fell
– Fell he said later, as if I stood ready,
'Into the strong arms of Thom Gunn.'
                                        Well well,
The image comic, as I might have known,
And generous, but it turned things round to myth:
He fell across the white steps there alone,
Though it was me indeed that he was with.

I hadn't caught him, hadn't seen in time,
And picked him up where he had softly dropped,
A pillow full of feathers. Was it a rime
He later sought, in which he might adopt
The role of H.D., broken-hipped and old,
Who, as she moved off from the reading-stand,
Had stumbled on the platform but was held
And steadied by another poet's hand?

He was now a posthumous poet, I have said
(For since his illness he had not composed),
In sight of a conclusion, whose great dread
Was closure,
                        his life soon to be enclosed
Like the sparrow's flight above the feasting friends,
Briefly revealed where its breast caught their light,
Beneath the long roof, between open ends,
Themselves the margins of unchanging night.

[182]

My Mother's Pride

She dramatized herself
Without thought of the dangers.
But 'Never pay attention,' she said,
'To the opinions of strangers.'

And when I stole from a counter,
'You wouldn't accept a present
From a tradesman.' But I think I might have:
I had the greed of a peasant.

She was proud of her ruthless wit
And the smallest ears in London.
'Only conceited children are shy.'
I am made by her, and undone.

The Gas-poker

Forty-eight years ago
– Can it be forty-eight
Since then? – they forced the door
Which she had barricaded
With a full bureau's weight
Lest anyone find, as they did,
What she had blocked it for.

She had blocked the doorway so,
To keep the children out.
In her red dressing-gown
She wrote notes, all night busy
Pushing the things about,
Thinking till she was dizzy,
Before she had lain down.

The children went to and fro
On the harsh winter lawn
Repeating their lament,
A burden, to each other
In the December dawn,
Elder and younger brother,
Till they knew what it meant.

Knew all there was to know.
Coming back off the grass
To the room of her release,
They who had been her treasures
Knew to turn off the gas,
Take the appropriate measures,
Telephone the police.

One image from the flow
Sticks in the stubborn mind:
A sort of backwards flute.
The poker that she held up
Breathed from the holes aligned
Into her mouth till, filled up
By its music, she was mute.

To Donald Davie in Heaven

I was reading Auden – But I thought
you didn't like Auden, I said.
Well, I've been reading him again,
and I like him better now, you said.
That was what I admired about you
your ability to regroup
without cynicism, your love of poetry
greater
than your love of consistency.

As in an unruffled fish-pond
the fish draw to whatever comes
thinking it something to feed on

there was always something to feed on
your appetite unslaked
for the fortifying and tasty
events of reading.

I try to think of you now
nestling in your own light,
as in Dante, singing to God
the poet and literary critic.

As you enter among them,
the other thousand surfaced glories
– those who sought honour
by bestowing it –

sing at your approach
Lo, one who shall increase our loves.

But maybe less druggy,
a bit plainer,
more Protestant.

The Artist as an Old Man

Vulnerable because
naked because
his own model.

Muscled and veined, not
a bad old body
for an old man.
The face vulnerable too,
its loosened folds
huddled against
the earlier outline: beneath
the assertion of nose
still riding the ruins
you observe the down-
turned mouth: and
above it,
the assessing glare
which might be read as
I've got the goods on you
asshole and I'll expose you.
The flat palette knife
in his right hand, and
the square palette itself
held low in the other
like a shield,
he faces off
the only appearance
reality has and makes it
doubly his. He

looks into
his own eyes
or it might be yours
and his attack on the goods
repeats the riddle
or it might be
answers it:
   *Out of the eater
      came forth meat
   and out of the strong
      came forth sweetness.*

A Wood near Athens

The traveler struggles through a wood. He is lost.
The traveler is at home. He never left.
He seeks his way on the conflicting trails,
Scribbled with light.
                              I have been this way before.

Think! the land here is wooded still all over.
An oak snatched Absalom by his bright hair.
The various trails of love had led him there,
The people's love, his father's, and self-love.

What if it does indeed come down to juices
And organs from whose friction we have framed
The obsession in which we live, obsession I call
The wood preceding us as we precede it?
We thought we lived in a garden, and looked around
To see that trees had risen on all sides.

2

It is ridiculous, ridiculous,
And it is our main meaning.
                              At some point
A biological necessity
Brought such a pressure on the human mind,
This concept floated from it – of a creator
Who made up matter, an imperfect world,
Solely to have an object for his love.

Beautiful and ridiculous. We say:
Love makes the shoots leap from the blunted branches,
Love makes birds call, and maybe we are right.
Love then makes craning saplings crowd for light,
The weak being jostled off to shade and death.
Love makes the cuckoo heave its foster-siblings
Out of the nest, to spatter on the ground.
For love has gouged a temporary hollow
Out of its baby-back, to help it kill.

But who did get it right? Ruth and Naomi,
Tearaway Romeo and Juliet,
Alyosha, Catherine Earnshaw, Jeffrey Dahmer?
They struggled through the thickets as they could.

A wedding entertainment about love
Was set one summer in a wood near Athens.
In paintings by Attila Richard Lukacs,
Cadets and skinheads, city boys, young Spartans
Wait poised like ballet-dancers in the wings
To join the balance of the corps in dances
Passion has planned. They that have power, or seem to,
They that have power to hurt, they are the constructs
Of their own longing, born on the edge of sleep,
Imperfectly understood.

                              Once a young man
Told me my panther made him think of one
His mother's boyfriend had on *his* forearm

– The first man he had sex with, at thirteen.
'Did she know about that?' I asked. He paused:
'I think so. Anyway, they were splitting up.'
'Were you confused?' – 'No, it was great,' he said,
'The best thing that had ever happened to me.'

And once, one looked above the wood and saw
A thousand angels making festival,
Each one distinct in brightness and in function,
Which was to choreograph the universe,
Meanwhile performing it. Their work was dance.
Together, wings outstretched, they sang and played
The intellect as powerhouse of love.

Dancing David

God

my darling and my daily ecstasy

I danced before the Lord, before the Ark,
I whirled and leapt, I danced with all my might,
     Uncovered in the sight
Of slaves and slavegirls, greeting the restored.
My dance was play and yet my play was work
That raised a homage to the appointing Lord.

I tasted sweat even though I wiped it off.
Beyond, I tasted all-approving air
     And cut swathes through it, where
Learning from it an indiscriminate taste
I drew all things to me, however rough,
The harvester in whom God's power is placed.

Saul's daughter watched me through the window-slit,
Despised me, took me for vulgarian,
     A vain and tasteless man.
She said 'How glorious was the King today.'
Ironic Michal, of the unkind wit,
Taste, taste, good taste will starve your years away.

For finicky taste will pucker up your womb
That shrinks in your disdain before the dance
        Of my uncouth advance,
Until it lose ability to swell,
No longer a capacious flexile room
But closed and empty like a light nutshell.

Bathsheba

Much later, in Jerusalem,
While I was walking on my roof
Above my people, watching them,
King, poet, close and yet aloof,

I glimpsed a certain woman nude,
I saw Bathsheba from above
Washing her breasts in solitude,
I learned the imperatives of love.

As for her husband, loyal fighter,
I had a kingly stratagem:
He was to carry me a letter,
All unaware it dealt with him.

I had him posted, for my ends,
In hottest battle of the line
And then abandoned by his friends,
So I could make Bathsheba mine.

Nothing to do, this time, with taste
But with the fervor of the dance
In which I kicked aside, from haste,
Any obstructing circumstance.

A common sequence, I observed:
Love leading to duplicity.
Displeasing to the lord I served,
Also, eventually, to me.

Yet from such commonness and greed
A wiser king than I was grown,
For in our very draining need
The seed of Solomon was sown.

Abishag

All my defiance in the past, I lay
Covered with bedclothes but I gat no heat.

They sought to take the chill off my old age
And found me the lithe virgin Abishag.

She lay on my bosom
                              oh pubescent girl
Smelling, how lightly, of anxiety,
The source of merely temporary mild heat
So innocent she might have been a dog.

Therefore Bathsheba handsomest of the wives
Entering my room came to the point at once,
Briskly demanding forthwith my assurance
Of the succession for her Solomon,
And took less notice of the girl than if
I had a closed pan of warm embers on me.

I relished secretly what I discovered,
Citron for a parched thought, Abishag
Sweet to the point of sharpness, dense and damp,
A comfort to the memory where I found,
Already present in the God-dance, her –
The ultimate moment of the improvisation,
A brief bow following on the final leap.

NOTES

Fighting Terms

First published by the Fantasy Press in 1954. In 1958 a revised
text, with two poems omitted, was published by the Hawk's
Well Press in New York. When it was eventually published by
Faber & Faber in 1961, the original text was mostly restored,
though the two rejected poems were still left out. FT was nearly
all written during G's period at Trinity College, Cambridge:
a remarkable achievement for an undergraduate. His failure
to revise the book proved instructive: he never again, to any
serious degree, tried to adapt the record. FT is marked by
what was to prove G's lasting enthusiasm for Elizabethan
poetry and drama. It was perhaps the most notable legacy of
the three years he spent reading English at Cambridge. Donne
and Shakespeare were at this time his twin enthusiasms, and
their influence runs all through the book, but it is Donne who
gives these poems their special character. 'Reading Donne was
a tremendous explosion for me, and I think a lot of that first
book . . . shows it . . . I think one thing Donne taught me was
what Frank Kermode calls the relationship between image
and discourse, and to be able to accept discourse as a proper
part of the poem in the twentieth century, as opposed to those
both in England and in America who thought that poetry was
entirely image' (JH, p. 36). As the title *Fighting Terms* suggests,
the key image in these early poems is that of the soldier. '[My]
childhood was full of soldiers . . . I was ten at the beginning
of World War Two and sixteen when it ended, so my visual
landscape was full of soldiers. Of course, I became a soldier
for two years of national service and so that was another
kind of soldier. It was a strange kind of role I had to measure
myself against' (PR, p. 155). In 1971 G noticed the book's

'Awkwardness and freshness' and his 'urgent desire to show off, both sexually and pedantically' (Bancroft 3:26).

'The Wound'
Composed at Cambridge, 1952.

G's version of the Trojan War is derived from Shakespeare's *Troilus and Cressida*, in which Achilles and Patroclus are represented as homosexual lovers. Sulking in his tent, Achilles observes that his inactivity has damaged his heroic reputation: 'My fame is shrewdly gored,' he says, and Patroclus replies, 'O then beware: / Those wounds heal ill that men do give themselves' (4.1.221–22). Thersites in Shakespeare's version is a cynical satirist. Neoptolemus (or Pyrrhus) was the son of Achilles; he avenged his father's death by burning Troy to the ground.

In the essay 'My Life up to Now', G writes of his soldier figure: 'First of all he is myself, the national serviceman, the "clumsy brute in uniform" [a quotation from G's "Captain in Time of Peace", not included in this selection], the soldier who never goes to war, whose role has no function, whose battledress is a joke. Secondly, though, he is a "real" soldier, both ideal and ambiguous, attractive and repellent: he is a warrior and a killer, or a career man in peace-time, or even a soldier on a quest like Odysseus or Sir Gawain . . . In . . . "The Wound" . . . the speaker is both – at one time Achilles, the real soldier in a real war, and at another time the self who dreamt he was Achilles' (OP, pp. 173–74).

G often said that 'The Wound' was the best poem in FT, though it 'seemed to me at the time rather mysterious, since I didn't acknowledge its sexual origins' (1971 notebook, Bancroft 3:26).

'Carnal Knowledge'
Composed during the long vacation, 1952.

The first edition of FT began with this poem. In subsequent editions, 'The Wound' was moved to the front.

There has been much discussion of G's 'Audenish custom of concealing the sex of a lover under the impersonal "you"' (WS, p. 11). This is certainly true of 'Tamer and Hawk', and such later poems as 'Touch', but G insisted that he never lied in his poems by deliberately suggesting that the addressee was a woman when it wasn't. 'Carnal Knowledge', he told W. I. Scobie, was 'addressed to a woman . . . I was making the most of the situation' (WS, p. 11). G comments on the refrain with its 'variations on the phrase "I know you know"' that 'anyone aware that I am a homosexual is likely to misread the whole poem, inferring that the thing "known" is that the speaker would prefer to be in bed with a man. But that would be a serious misreading, or at least a serious misplacement of emphasis. The poem, actually addressed to a fusion of two completely different girls, is not saying anything as clear-cut as that. A reader knowing nothing about the author has a much better chance of understanding it' (OP, p. 188).

G copied the poem into a letter to his friend Karl Miller. He tells Miller that, working at a fruit-picking camp, he had met a young woman who was attracted to him.

> I have written a poem which I enclose: it is founded on real life, as you shall see . . . Round about the 3rd evening I became involved with a girl called Ann – at first sight something very attractive about her. A kiss became prolonged and the situation became inescapable. I felt very vigorous during the first week or 2 and was prepared to experiment

without stop, and while we still had confidence in each other and there was still exploration to be made everything was well . . . She never, I am convinced, suspected for a minute that I loved men, and I was very nice to her. She said at the very beginning that as she was a Roman Catholic she would not have intercourse with me: however it was obvious I cd persuade her to in a few days.

But tho I was very interested until my curiosity was satisfied mere curiosity is soon satisfied, and I never for a minute imagined I felt any passion. To my credit, I never pretended to be more than casual. I carried off casualness with panache for a while; but I began to get bored, & there is also a feeling of <u>fear</u> of being committed to an attitude one does not sincerely feel so I had to make the necessary break, and I now see I was more unkind than I had meant to be. I knew that I cd have persuaded her to do anything I wanted – but I would not have been adequate to deal with her afterwards . . .

[Two heterosexual male friends] . . . are at present trying to persuade me to make love to a dear little girl from Leeds whom they assure me has indicated I would not be disagreeable – you would think her very lovely, and she is – but I have learnt by the affair with Ann that one must not enter on such things if one cannot be happy in them and make the girl happy.

(KM, 14 July 1952)

This makes it very clear that the posture of cynical misogyny borrowed from Donne is a fabrication, though it may represent the behaviour he imagines the hurt girl to have experienced.

Line 9: cf. 'Unaccommodated man is no more but such a poor, bare, forked animal as thou art' (*King Lear*, 3.4.100–01).

Line 21: i.e. the heart: a commonplace of Elizabethan poetry.
Cf. 'the space / Between the breast and lips – Tiberius' heart'
(Ben Jonson, *Sejanus*, 3.1.2011–12).

Line 32: cf. 'If you have tears, prepare to shed them now'
(*Julius Caesar*, 3.2.166).

'Lerici'
Composed 1953.

Shelley spent much of 1822 at San Terenzo, near Lerici, in
the Bay of Spezia. On 8 July he was drowned when his boat
capsized in a squall; there is an apocryphal story that he gave
himself up to death. A week later, he was cremated on a beach
near Viareggio, where his body had been washed ashore. After
the funeral, Byron swam out to his own yacht and back, a
distance of some three miles. A famously powerful swimmer,
he once swam the Hellespont in emulation of the legendary
Leander, who had swum that distance every night to visit his
mistress, Hero.

G's representation of Shelley may have something to do
with the notoriously negative view of him taken by F. R.
Leavis – self-indulgent, self-pitying, preferring death to life.
See the essay on Shelley in Leavis's *Revaluation: Tradition and
Development in English Poetry* (1936). Leavis's intolerance of
self-pity troubled G throughout his life. G saw it as a necessary
if unattractive emotion (see note to 'Innocence', pp. 216–18).

'Tamer and Hawk'
Written at Cambridge for Mike Kitay, spring 1953. First published in the New Statesman and Nation, *14 November 1953, it was G's second professional publication.*

Shakespeare and other Elizabethan authors were fond of images taken from the sport of falconry. These are often metaphors for aspects of the war of the sexes. Petruchio in *The Taming of the Shrew*, for instance, tames his termagant wife, Katharina, much as a falconer will tame a hawk. 'To seel' a hawk is to close its eyes by stitching up its eyelids: this is part of the taming process. See T. H. White, *The Goshawk* (1951), a book G may have read around this time.

'Incident on a Journey'
Composed 1953.

This poem may be indebted to Robert Louis Stevenson's *Kidnapped*, a story of the Jacobite rebellions, which G admired as a boy, though in later life he remembered no connection. He *did* borrow from *Kidnapped* in 'Jack Straw's Castle', though (see p. 244 below). The bond between the inexperienced Calvinist Lowlander David Balfour and the Romantic Jacobite rebel Alan Breck, around which the novel is built, might be read as a homoerotic friendship. Furthermore, the characters seem two sides of the same coin, which might recall the divided selves of 'The Wound' and other early poems of G's.

The Sense of Movement

Published by Faber & Faber in 1957. This was the first of
G's collections to be written in the United States, much of it
showing the influence of G's teacher at Stanford University,
the poet and critic Yvor Winters. 'The poems make much use
of the word "will". It was a favourite word of [Jean-Paul]
Sartre's, and one that Winters appreciated, but they each meant
something very different by it, and would have understood but
not admitted the other's use of it. What *I* meant was, ultimately,
a mere Yeatsian wilfulness' (OP, p. 177). In an interview G said
that he had not yet realised when he wrote the book that, for
Shakespeare and his contemporaries, 'will' was the colloquial
word for 'penis': 'I was getting it unconsciously' (PR, pp. 154–
55).

   SM includes many of G's most frequently anthologised
poems. It was in this book that he began creating the myth of
the motorcyclist as unconscious existentialist and admitting the
influence of popular culture, as in 'Elvis Presley', for example.
Writing of the French poet Charles Baudelaire (1821–67),
one of the key influences on his early work, G commented:
'Baudelaire's ennui has now become democratic – it is no
longer the poet's prerogative. It has become a wider and at the
same time more undefined malaise . . .', and he goes on to cite
'the hoodlums in some of my poems like "On the Move" . . .'
(sleeve note to the LP *On The Move*, released by *Listen*, 1962).
As the years passed, however, he came to dislike the book
for (as he saw it) its excessive formality and over-deliberate
manner: 'A lot of it seems very stiff,' he wrote in 1971 (Bancroft
3:26). He eventually came to prefer FT, much less accomplished
though he knew it to be.

'On the Move'
Composed spring 1955.

'I was much taken by the American myth of the motorcyclist, then in its infancy, of the wild man part free spirit and part hoodlum . . .' (OP, p.177). More immediately, the poem was inspired by Laslo Benedek's film *The Wild One* (1954), which starred the young Marlon Brando as an anarchic biker. It originally bore an epigraph from the film: 'Man you gotta go.' The philosophy of personal freedom is directly taken from a short book of Jean-Paul Sartre's, *L'Existentialisme est un humanisme* (1946): 'I certainly kept close to that text the year or two I was writing SM' (JH, p. 36).

It is undoubtedly G's best-known poem. He was originally very proud of it: 'This . . . is the only time I have written adequately on one of the really important subjects: the poem is about movement as an experiment, and about "the search for value" as a value in itself' ('Four Young Poets – IV: Thom Gunn', *TES* 2150, 3 August 1956, p. 995). He came in later life to dislike it, for the use of 'one' rather than 'you', 'which I find very stilted now', 'because of its tremendous formality' and because he was 'not sure that the last line means anything' (JC, p. 29).

Line 32: G wrote: 'most English people nowadays give "toward" two syllables, whereas Americans, like the Elizabethans, treat it as one. In my early books I was still an English poet, not yet Anglo-American' (CP, p. 489).

'At the Back of the North Wind'
Composed while at Stanford, 1954.

The title is that of a prose romance by George MacDonald (1824–1905), a Victorian writer for children, whose books G enjoyed as a boy. The book's first chapter is called 'The Hayloft'.

'Autumn Chapter in a Novel'
Composed 1954–55.

The hero and his amorous adventures recall those of Julien Sorel in Stendhal's novel *Le Rouge et le noir*. Stendhal (1783–1842) was one of G's favourite novelists and Stendhal's heroes, Julien and Fabrice (in *La Chartreuse de Parme*), came to represent for G the man who lives by the will. As a young man, G thought that 'everyone plays a part, whether he knows it or not, so he might as well deliberately design a part, or a series of parts, for himself. Only a psychopath or a very good actor is in danger of *becoming* his part, however, so one who is neither is left in an interesting place between the starting point – the bare undefined and undirected self, if he ever existed – and the chosen part. This is a place rich in tensions between the achieved and the unachieved. I thought of Julien Sorel with Madame Rénal [Julien's aristocratic mistress], the counterpoint a man's vulnerable emotions made upon his seduction timed by the clock' (OP, p. 162).

   G suggested to his editor, Charles Monteith, that this poem might be included in *Selected Poems* of Thom Gunn and Ted Hughes, to make a contrast with poems like 'On the Move': 'so as to show I can be well-turned, ironic, detached, and all

NOTES TO PAGES 20–21

that jazz . . .' (F&F, 19 September 1961). G said with reference to 'Autumn Chapter in a Novel' that he 'admired the kind of poem where meaning is achieved through the images, through a description – something which could be reducible to a statement but the statement isn't made anywhere' (JH, p. 41).

'The Silver Age'
Composed 1964.

The Golden Age is traditionally the age of innocence, identified with sunlight and pastoral harmony. The Silver Age, therefore, reminds us of moonlight and inwardness. Cf. 'For Signs' and contrast 'Sunlight' in Gunn's *Moly*, pp. 88–89 and 98–99 below.

Livy – Titus Livius (59 BC–AD 17) – wrote a monumental history of Rome in 142 books, of which only 32 survive.

The poem appears to be a not wholly successful attempt to write in accentual verse.

'Elvis Presley'
Composed in San Antonio, Texas, 1955, after hearing a Presley record on a jukebox.

'[T]he poem is about the young Elvis Presley . . . of "Hound Dog" and "Heartbreak Hotel"' (JC, p. 29). He described the poem as saying 'that art is one of the ways in which we can overcome the inadequacies of the condition we find ourselves living in' (JH, p. 40).

'The Allegory of the Wolf Boy'
Composed 1956.

Probably a response to the contemporary fashion for horror films such as *The Werewolf* (1956) and *I was a Teenage Werewolf* (1957). G confirmed in conversation that the poem was about growing up as a gay youth and feeling compelled to live a double life.

'Jesus and his Mother'
Composed before leaving England, 1954.

The 'garden ripe with pears' suggests a fifteenth-century Italian painting, such as by the Venetian artist Carlo Crivelli (d. 1495/1500). Compare 'Expression' (p. 129).

'To Yvor Winters, 1955'
Composed at Stanford, 1955–56.

Winters (1900–68) is best known as a fiercely combative literary critic with a powerful code of stoical humanism. G admired such critical books as his *In Defense of Reason* (1947) but valued his poetry still more. In 1966 G listed the modern poets he most admired as Pound, Hardy and William Carlos Williams. 'Eliot, Winters, Lowell etc,' he continued, 'come slightly lower – they do not experience so directly. On the other hand, they do try to understand their experience – which I suppose as a human being one ought to do – but the attempt to understand removes some of the vividness of the experience' (TT, 5 May 1966). In other comparable lists he included Wallace Stevens and D. H. Lawrence. The emphasis on understanding is something he shared with Winters.

The conflict between direct experience and considered reflection, central to Winters's poetry and criticism, runs all through G's work. It accounts for the contrasts in his versification and for the emphasis in the late work on openness and closure (see 'Duncan', pp. 181–82). In 1999 he edited Winters's *Selected Poems* for the Library of America and elsewhere described him as 'a man of great personal warmth with a deeper love of poetry than I have ever met in anybody else' (OP, p. 176). He also thought Winters a great teacher, though as he developed he grew wary of him 'from something of an instinct for self-preservation. The man was too strong . . .' (OP, p. 178).

Winters bred Airedale terriers for competition and admired the great boxer Joe Louis. In the introduction to his last book, Winters eloquently compares 'the poet to the breeder of dogs and to the boxer, and the critic to the judge of both' (*Forms of Discovery*, Athens, OH: Alan Swallow, 1967, xix).

'Vox Humana'
Composed 1956–57.

Latin: 'the human voice'. It is also the name for one of the stops on an organ. The poem, however, is a kind of riddle, to which the answer must be something like destiny, or even identity.

Alexander the Great, a heroic figure with homosexual associations, was a preoccupation of G's; he is G's persona in 'From an Asian Tent' (p. 47). Sentenced to death for corrupting the young, Socrates was obliged to take hemlock, which is a poison. The ghost of Caesar appeared to his assassin, Marcus

Brutus, before the Battle of Philippi (42 BC), to anticipate his defeat and death. The encounter is enacted in *Julius Caesar* 4.2. This list of classical heroes – mostly filtered through Shakespeare's Greek and Roman plays – relates to another poem in SM, 'A Plan of Self-Subjection' (CP, p. 46):

> As Alexander or Mark Antony
> Or Coriolanus, whom I most admire,
> I mask self-flattery.

'Vox Humana' is one of G's first experiments in syllabic metre, in which the syllables are counted but not the accents or feet.

My Sad Captains

Published by Faber & Faber in 1961. The book is in two parts.
'The first is the culmination of my old style – metrical and
rational but maybe starting to get a little more humane. The
second half consists of a taking up of that humane impulse in a
series of poems in syllabics' (OP, p. 179). Part I has an epigraph
adapted from *Troilus and Cressida*: 'The will is infinite and the
execution confined, the desire is boundless and the act a slave
to limit' (3.2.79–82). The epigraph to Part II is from F. Scott
Fitzgerald's *The Last Tycoon*: 'I looked back as we crossed the
crest of the foothills – with the air so clear you could see the
leaves on Sunset Mountains two miles away. It's startling to
you sometimes – just air, unobstructed, uncomplicated air.' G
attributed his change of manner in the second section to the
influence of William Carlos Williams. In the syllabic poems, he
said, 'I found a way, with Williams' help, of incorporating the
more casual aspects of life, the non-heroic things in life, that
are of course a part of daily experience and infinitely valuable'
(PR, p. 151). See G's essay 'A New World: The Poetry of
William Carlos Williams' (OP, pp. 21–35).

   G claimed that writing in syllabic verse was 'a way of
teaching myself about unpatterned rhythms – that is, about
free verse' (OP, p. 179). He learned much about the distinction
between free verse and metre from an essay by D. H. Lawrence:
'It seems to me that the freer forms – and that includes syllabics
– are hospitable to improvisation or the feel of improvisation.
Lawrence . . . speaks of free verse as poetry of the present: that
is, it grabs in the details and these are probably very casual
details of the present, of whatever is floating though the air,
whatever is on the table at the time, whatever is underfoot,

however trivial – trivial but meaningful. Whereas metrical verse, he says . . . has the greater finish, because in a sense it deals with events or experience or thinking that are more finished. Finished in both senses: in a punning sense, it's also more over and done with. He calls it "poetry of the past"' (PR, p. 165). In another context he says that the poems are 'more open to the sensory, to the process of life rather than the meaning of life' (Bancroft 3:26). (For the Lawrence essay, see also Introduction, pp. xxxi–xxxii.) It was not until such poems as 'Yoko' (pp. 123–25) that G attempted a free-verse line comparable to Lawrence's or to that of Lawrence's master, Walt Whitman.

In an unpublished interview of 1959, he compared the themes of this book with his earlier themes: 'Alvarez said that the theme of my first book was "doubt" and that of my second "choice". What comes after "choice"? . . . Well, I think, and hope, it will be "conduct".'

'In Santa Maria del Popolo'
Composed 1958. (Gunn had spent several months in Rome in 1954.)

The setting is a sixteenth-century church in the Piazza del Popolo in Rome. It contains two frescos by Michelangelo da Caravaggio (1573–1610), one of them a Conversion of St Paul, depicted in dramatic chiaroscuro. In the Acts of the Apostles, Saul of Tarsus is a Jewish leader who persecutes Christians. Struck down by a vision on the Damascus road, he is converted to Christianity. In sign of the change in his life he changes his name to Paul. For Ananias and other details of the story see Acts 9.1–20.

Caravaggio's paintings, including those G alludes to, are often marked by homosexual feeling, and his life seems to have been short and dramatic. At the time of his death he was busy avoiding arrest for murder. He died young and in mysterious circumstances, though, as G later realised, there is no evidence for the legend of his death referred to here.

When he wrote MSC, G had begun to see the limitations to his idea of the heroic. As he observed, this poem notices not only St Paul but 'the poor old women praying in the chapel. So that to some extent I've gone out into the world, away from the first two books and the blustering heroism of people who are self-regarding. I praised and exalted such people as if there were no other way of getting outside oneself . . . Getting outside oneself was one of the things I learned from Williams . . .' (JH, p. 42).

'Innocence'
Composed in Berlin, 1960.

G was much preoccupied with innocence. For a positive account of innocence, see 'Three' (pp. 90–91) and the note to it (p. 236).

G said that the story of this poem was taken from 'a book called *Autobiography of an SS Man*, translated by Constantine FitzGibbon, which showed how somebody who began as a humane person could commit an atrocity. I dedicated it to Tony White . . . since we had discussed this kind of thing' (JH, p. 45). 'I should point out that dedicating a poem to someone does not necessarily mean that it is about him' (CP, p. 490). For Tony White, see Introduction (p. xxvi), the poem 'Talbot Road' (pp. 144–50) and the note for it (pp. 252–53).

G composed the poem in Berlin. It took an exceptionally long time to write because it gave expression to so many moral problems. G attempted to justify it in a long letter to Tony Tanner, who had criticised an early draft of it:

In it I'm trying to deal with a problem I've never before fully faced in a poem, the problem of the consequences of energy (which I admire) without moral sanction.

No, I am not trying to sell the SS man as something fine in his own way. But I am trying to show how like he is to most people, or rather how easy it would be for most people to (in the right circumstances) be in the SS . . . I think there is ultimately rather little difference, in war, between the attitude a soldier has toward killing (which is never clean, a neat hole thro the forehead) and that he has toward atrocity. By attributing innocence to this man I am not exonerating him or the SS, but I <u>am</u> attacking innocence.

In the first 3 stanzas, I am deliberately keeping myself from judging <u>against</u> the boy (except in the line about 'hardening to an instrument' which is more against the SS than him), because I am trusting the last two stanzas to do the work for me. Surely those 2 stanzas show that the 'courage, endurance, loyalty, and skill' are virtues meaning nothing without the virtue of wisdom (vide. Plato passim), and that innocence is <u>not</u>, as popularly supposed, a virtue, but a mere vacancy, into which anything can be put, including horrors.

Lines 6–7: '. . . guilt's vague heritage / Self-pity and the soul . . .' Though G was attracted to stoicism and so not especially prone to self-pity, he was nevertheless preoccupied with it. Of Ben Jonson's poem 'Ode to Himselfe', he wrote: 'It is a poem of self-pity, and (in spite of all that I was taught at Cambridge) self-pity is something people feel often enough for it to be a subject worth writing about' (OP, p. 115). As James Campbell points out in his interview with G, the reference to Cambridge here is striking. G is thinking of the very moralistic literary criticism which he admired at university, especially that of F. R. Leavis: 'Anybody who took Leavis's lectures will remember the way he'd say "self-pit-teh" when talking about, let's say, some poem by Shelley – "Ode to the West Wind", perhaps . . . I think he thought self-pity was a limitation in moral fibre' (JC, p. 23). But as G would point out in conversation, if you can't feel sorry for yourself, you probably can't feel sorry for others either. Moral failure of that kind is the subject of this poem, which is very much a critique of G's earlier attitudes, heroic, stoical, existentialist or Leavisite. Of the gentler, more humanistic self that emerges in MSC, he said jokingly: 'I was less of a fascist. I had been a Shakespearean, Sartrean fascist!' (PR, p. 165).

'Modes of Pleasure'
Composed 1960. Originally titled 'With Good Humor'.

There are two poems with this title in MSC, both of them about sexual adventurers. G said they were 'about going to the leather bars': 'I was reading the poems of Rochester [John Wilmot, Earl of Rochester, a major poet of the seventeenth century] at the time I wrote "Modes of Pleasure," so that might have something to do with it. I saw this poem as being a bit like Rochester's, though they probably aren't at all [alike]. Rochester made himself out to be bisexual, but I think that was only to shock. Most of his poetry is sexual, even pornographic' (CH).

'The Byrnies'
Composed 1957–58.

The heroes are Viking invaders. G wrote: 'a byrnie is a chainmail shirt; a nicker was a water monster' (CP, p. 490). Rereading William Golding's *The Inheritors* in 1962, G realised that this poem 'owes a lot in conception' to Golding's book (F&F, 25 August 1962). In 1971 he thought it 'as good as I have got' (Bancroft 3:26).

'Claus von Stauffenberg'
Composed 1958.

Von Stauffenberg (1907–44) was the leader of the conspiracy to assassinate Hitler in 1944. When the plot failed, he was arrested and executed. The analogy with Brutus (line 16) derives from Shakespeare's *Julius Caesar*, with its portrait of the idealistic assassin. Shakespeare's Roman plays had an enormous influence on G's youthful sense of stoical heroism. Cf. 'Epitaph for Anton Schmidt' in 'Misanthropos', pp. 70–71.

Line 13: 'The maimed young Colonel.' Stauffenberg had lost his right hand and all but two of the fingers on his left.

Line 17: 'Over the maps a moment.' Stauffenberg planted his bomb while attending a briefing given by Hitler and senior Nazi leaders. There were maps on the table.

'Flying Above California'
Composed 1960.

After six years in the United States, G was becoming a regional poet, as much a Californian as Wordsworth was a Cumbrian. (Cf. 'Night Taxi', pp. 151–53. In both poems the proper names are crucial.)

'Considering the Snail'
Completed 1960. First called 'The Snail'.

G used to say that this poem was inspired by a painting of Paul Klee's which he saw in reproduction. The work in question is almost certainly *Snail* (1924), a painting in tempera on paper in the Museo Cantonale d'Arte, Lugano. Klee's snail undoubtedly 'pushes through a green / night'.

'The Feel of Hands'
Composed 1958.

This poem anticipates one of G's masterpieces, 'Touch' (pp. 56–57).

'My Sad Captains'
Composed 1961.

When Mark Antony loses the battle of Actium and knows that he has lost the struggle for power, he summons his generals and friends to a last revel:

> Come,
> Let's have one other gaudy night. Call to me
> All my sad captains. Fill our bowls once more.

Let's mock the midnight bell.
(*Antony and Cleopatra*, 4.2.184–87)

'Sad' in Shakespeare's English means 'grave' or 'serious'. The
title was suggested by G's partner, Mike Kitay. G regarded this
as one of his best poems. Speaking of its syllabic form, he said:
'I think I hit on something there but it's not something I've
been able to repeat. There's something going on there with the
sounds that I'm amazed I was able to achieve. I don't think
I've ever done that in free verse . . . I certainly couldn't do it in
meter: it's not a metrical effect' (PR, pp. 166–67).

Uncollected

'From an Asian Tent'
Composed 1961.

Completed too late to be published in *My Sad Captains* (1961), this poem seems not to have fitted into G's next collection, *Touch* (1967). It was eventually reprinted in a pamphlet, *The Missed Beat* (Newark, VT: Janus, 1976), and was subsequently included in G's *Collected Poems*.

In a notebook of 1972, G writes: 'Like most homosexuals, I disliked my father, tho I have since learned to have a certain sympathy for him' (notebook for autobiography, 1972, Bancroft). In 'From an Asian Tent', he writes elsewhere, 'I am finally able to write about my father . . . I would like the poem to be read as being about what it proclaims as its subject: Alexander the Great remembering [his father] Philip of Macedon. What is autobiographical about the poem, what I am drawing upon, is a secret source of feeling that might really be half-imagined, some Oedipal jealousy for my father combined with a barely remembered but equally strong incestuous desire for him. And I am drawing upon the autobiographical without scruple, freed by the myth from any attempt to be fair or honest about my father. The poem's truth is in its faithfulness to a possibly imagined feeling, not to my history' (OP, pp. 187–88).

Herbert Gunn died in 1962, the year after the poem was written.

Positives

Published by Faber & Faber in 1965. The book is a
collaboration between G and his photographer brother, Ander.
This collection was never intended as a major book of poetry,
but as a set of photographs with verse captions. It records
with evident pleasure a year G spent in London: 1964–65
(see 'Talbot Road', pp. 144–50). The poems follow the course
of human life from birth to death: 'a friend of ours jokingly
referred to it as "the Gunn Brothers' Guide to Humans"' (F&F,
26 August 1965). In this book G for the first time abandoned
rhyme in syllabics and then moved on to free verse. There are
no titles in the book; the one I have given is from G's *Poems
1950–1966: A Selection*.

'The Old Woman'
Composed in London, 1965.

Ander Gunn's photograph shows an extremely old woman,
clearly a derelict, across the way from G's flat in Talbot Road
in the Notting Hill district of London. The notable graininess
of the picture seems to symbolise the process of gradual
decomposition that is the poem's chief concern. G had this
picture framed with a holograph of the poem underneath it. It
used to hang on the first landing of his San Francisco home.

Touch

Published by Faber & Faber in 1967. In the six years between MSC and *Touch*, G changed and experimented a great deal. He seems to have been uncertain of his direction and dismissed *Touch*, the product of this uncertainty, as the only one of his books to have bored most of his readers. When he published CP in 1993, he replaced *Touch* with a section entitled 'Poems from the 1960s', which selected from the book and added a few uncollected ones. Despite that, I have decided to retain the title *Touch* for the historical record.

In *Touch*, as in *Positives*, unrhymed syllabics appear alongside early attempts at free verse, including the title poem. G learned the technique of free verse from an essay by Yvor Winters, 'The Scansion of Free Verse', and in particular from Winters's analysis of William Carlos Williams's poem 'By the road to the contagious hospital' (later called 'Spring and All'). In that poem, says G in a summary, there is 'usually an even number of major stresses to the line, with lines ending as often as possible in mid-phrase' (TT, 12 August ?1966). See Winters, *In Defense of Reason* (London: Routledge, 1962), pp. 112–29. Winters's method also allows for a certain number of secondary stresses not counted in the scansion.

Commenting on the title, G wrote: 'the touch is not physical only, it is meant to be an allegory for the touch of sympathy that should be the aim of human intercourse. The man in . . . "Misanthropos" at last discovers it, though he has in the past substituted for it the predatory bite of the animal.' A poem not included here, 'Confessions of the Life Artist', was intended, says G, 'to summarise the nightmare of any civilized man, as the end of "Misanthropos" is meant to summarise his dream,

[224]

because one has to seek the fullness of control if one wants to avoid sloth; but it seems that the more controlled one is the more unfit one becomes for the spontaneity of "touch", which is the only real proof, in a human anyway, of unslothfulness. The celebration of instinct in . . . "The Goddess", is all very well, but instinct is self-protective and predatory and it defeats the exercise of sympathy just as much as the over-self-consciousness of the Life Artist. There remains the possibility that one can deliberately and consciously attempt to create in oneself a field which will be spontaneously fertile for the tests of sympathy, that one can form habits that are so readily available that they seem like instincts' (*Poetry Book Society Bulletin*, September 1967). G subsequently mocked the 'cumbersome' prose of this passage, but it articulates, however laboriously, the moral issues that occupied him for most of his life.

'The Goddess'
Composed 1961.

'I used to believe my muse was male; but I've come to realize that [Robert] Graves is right, that the muse has to be female. The Goddess is a mother, not a wife or a lover. The feminine principle is the source and I think it dominates in male artists whether homo- or heterosexual' (WS, p. 15). There now seems no doubt that G's Muse was either his mother or a figure projected out of her. See e.g. 'Rites of Passage' (p. 85).

Line 22: Proserpina (Greek: Persephone) is the Roman Goddess of Spring, the renewal of life and the crop cycle. She is also, as the wife of Pluto, the Goddess of Death and Queen of the Underworld. In view of G's relationship with his mother

NOTES TO PAGES 56–79

and her suicide, these traditions are deeply significant.

'Touch'
Composed 1966.

This poem about falling asleep should be read alongside a
poem about waking up, John Donne's 'The Good-Morrow'.
It is also related to Robert Creeley's 'The World', which
must have influenced its versification and which is brilliantly
discussed in G's essay on Creeley, 'Small Persistent Difficulties'
(SL, pp. 91–95). Surprisingly, in that context, G wrote: 'It has a
good deal to do with reading, and trying to like, Edward Dorn,
I think' (TT, 13 September 1966).
  'Continuous creation' is one of the theories of the origin
of the universe, sometimes called the 'steady-state theory', in
which the universe has no beginning and no end.

'Misanthropos'
*Begun in San Francisco in 1963, possibly earlier, and completed
in London, January 1965. It was broadcast on the BBC Third
Programme (8 March 1965) and published in the magazine*
Encounter *(August 1965).*

G had already written a good deal of this sequence when he
came to London on a year-long scholarship in Autumn 1964.
He worked on it off and on during those first months. It is
worth noting that during the same scholarship year he also
wrote the poems for *Positives*, his long essay 'A New World:
The Poetry of William Carlos Williams' and another sequence,
not included here, 'Confessions of the Life Artist'. He also

edited the *Selected Poems* of Fulke Greville for Faber & Faber
and wrote his superb introduction for it.

'Misanthropos' 'began as a single poem about a man who
finds himself the last survivor of a nuclear holocaust' (WS,
p. 12). G described it as part pastoral, part science fiction.
'The narrative owes a lot to . . . my friends Don Doody and
Tony Tanner [the literary critic]. I had been recovering from
a bout of hepatitis, and listening to them discussing ideas
and books and things, and quite a bit of their discussion later
appeared in the poem' (WS, pp. 12–13). The illness no doubt
had its effect on section X, though G was more consciously
drawing on microscopic images of growing cancer cells. The
literary sources are manifold. The moral outlook of the poem,
especially as represented in 'Epitaph for Anton Schmidt' (pp.
70–71), is indebted to Albert Camus, particularly to the figure
of Dr Rieux in *La Peste* (*The Plague*, 1947), though in an
interview G was more inclined to stress Camus's *La Chute*
(*The Fall*, 1956), 'which was on my mind in the section called
"Memoirs of the World", where the hero looks back on his
past, just as the hero of *La Chute* is constantly looking back'
(JH, p. 44). Shakespeare's *Timon of Athens*, which G rated
more highly than is customary, and *King Lear* provide the
image of the misanthrope who has withdrawn to the desert
and attempts to answer the question 'What is man?' Sir
Philip Sidney's *Arcadia*, a source of *King Lear*, is also there,
as is Sidney's inspiration, the *Eclogues* of Virgil. For other
images of isolation, see Franz Kafka's story 'The Burrow' in
Metamorphosis and Daniel Defoe's *Robinson Crusoe*. The
most important contemporary influence was probably William
Golding. His novel *Pincher Martin* (1956), which evokes a
man's struggle to survive on a rock in the Atlantic, represents
a critical response to Defoe's account of human nature. There

are also touches from Golding's *Lord of the Flies* (1954), which is about survivors of a nuclear war, and, as G was glad to acknowledge, *The Inheritors* (1955), an extraordinary feat of imagination depicting the demise of Neanderthal man. In *The Inheritors*, the last man (a Neanderthaler) encounters a tribe of *Homo sapiens*, who are, in another sense, the 'first' men. Writing to his and Golding's publisher, Charles Monteith, at some time in the 1960s, G declares of Golding's novel: 'God, what a beautiful book that is! Golding is one of the few living novelists who make me wish I weren't a poet but a novelist' (F&F, 25 August 1962).

For the importance of 'Misanthropos' to the collection *Touch*, see headnote (p. 224).

The title. From Shakespeare's *Timon of Athens*, 4.3.49–54:

Alcibiades:	What art thou there? Speak.
Timon:	A beast as thou art. The canker gnaw thy heart,
	For showing me again the eyes of man!
Alcibiades:	What is thy name? Is man so hateful to thee That art thyself a man?
Timon:	I am *Misanthropos*, and hate mankind.

I. Written in conscious imitation of Wallace Stevens with his 'Ideas of Order' and imagination.

II. An echo poem. This is a Renaissance genre, which is found, for instance, in such musical works as Claudio Monteverdi's *Vespers* of 1610. G's immediate sources are the Second Eclogue from Sidney's *The Old Arcadia* and George Herbert's poem 'Heaven'. Herbert's poem, for instance, ends with these lines:

Then tell me, what is that supreme delight?
      Echo   *Light.*
Light to the minde: what shall the will enjoy?
      Echo.   *Joy.*
But are there cares and businesse with the pleasure?
      Echo.   *Leisure.*
Light, joy, and leisure; but shall they persever?
      Echo.   *Ever.*

VI. A reminiscence of G's boyhood, based 'on picking up wood on Hampstead Heath during the war . . .' (TT, undated, prob. 1965).

IX. Soon after completing this section, G wrote: 'I adore this poem, and don't know how I wrote it' (TT, undated, prob. 1965). For the opening, see *King Lear*, 3.4.83, where Edgar speaks in the role of the mad beggar Poor Tom:

Lear: What hast thou been?
Edgar: A serving-man, proud in heart and mind,
               that curled my hair, wore gloves in my cap,
               served the lust of my mistress' heart and did
               the act of darkness with her . . .

XI. 'This is [with IX] the other one I like. It's a bit like my poem on Claus von Stauffenberg, but I think it replaces it rather than being parasitic on it' (TT, undated, prob. 1965). 'I found Anton Schmidt in Hannah Arendt's *Eichmann in Jerusalem*' (CP, p. 490).
    Line 2: *Feldwebel*: 'sergeant' in German. G had himself been a sergeant in the Royal Army Education Corps.
    Line 6: 'Reposeful and humane good nature' is Herman Melville's description of his Billy Budd.

XII. G took the form of this elegy from Andrew Marvell's 'The Mower against Gardens', which 'alternates pentameter and tetrameter lines rhyming in couplets' (JH, p. 44). It is also indebted to George Herbert's 'Church Monuments', a poem much admired by Yvor Winters (TT, undated, prob. 1965).

XIII. 'This is plagiaristic of [William] Golding's The Inheritors and of [Thomas] Mann's The Holy Sinner: do you care? Does the start read like a parody of T. S. Eliot?' (TT, undated, 1965).

'Pierce Street'
Composed 1966.

The title refers to a street in San Francisco. The house in question belonged to one of G's gay, druggy friends, Jere Fransway, who was to be (at a later stage in life) the subject of 'Falstaff' in 'Transients and Residents' (pp. 137–38). The house had been decorated by another member of their group, probably Chuck Arnett – 'Crystal' in the same sequence (pp. 138–39).

G liked 'the pretty effects of the rhymes' in this poem: 'Borrowed from Pound! Who got it from Cavalcanti!' (TT, June 1966). Guido Cavalcanti (c.1255–1300) was a major influence upon Dante and the finest poet among Dante's friends and contemporaries. He was much admired and frequently translated by Ezra Pound (see note to 'The Differences', pp. 258–60).

Moly

Published by Faber & Faber in 1971. To the end of his life,
G thought *Moly* 'unquestionably my best book' (Bancroft
3:26). It arose primarily from his and his friends' experiences
of taking the drug LSD. The book begins with a condensed
quotation from Homer's *Odyssey*, in which Hermes gives
Odysseus the herb called moly to protect him against the
sorceress Circe, who has turned his sailors into pigs. 'I see Moly
as the antidote to the piggishness in man (some might see it as
the thorazine to be used for an acid freak-out, but let it be, that
ambiguity) . . . Alternative title. SUNSHINE. For: it covers the
sunlight imagery that is suppose[d] to grow during the book,
and it is also coming, more and more, to be a synonym for
acid . . .' (TT, 22 April 1970). 'LSD . . . extends your awareness
into other areas. It's chemical: it may be simply that you're not
aware of seeing round corners but you just think you are. You
tend to think that these other areas are spiritual – and they may
be' (PR p. 166).

The book was strongly influenced in theme, if not in method,
by Ezra Pound and, through Pound, by the *Metamorphoses*
of Ovid, one of the masterpieces of the Latin language, the
subjects of which are change, mutability and transformation.
'[T]he whole theme of the book is metamorphosis . . . That
was LSD, of course. It did make you into a different person.
The myths of metamorphosis had much more literal meaning
for me: the idea that somebody could grow horns [in "Rites
of Passage"], that somebody could grow into a laurel tree, or
that somebody could be a centaur . . . or turn into an angel. In
the hallucinations – or more likely, distortions – that you saw
under the influence of LSD, things did change their shape' (PR,

p. 168). '[T]he main subject of my book' is 'change, whether with the help of drugs or not, as a result of a recognition. A recognition is always itself the start of a change – is a change in itself' (Bancroft Ctn. 3:18). G also remarked that the book had other themes besides metamorphosis: 'It could be seen as a debate between the passion for definition and the passion for flow, it could be seen as a history of San Francisco from 1965–9, or as a personal memoir of myself during those years' (Bancroft 3:21).

The book is also preoccupied with sunlight as the primary source of energy. In a letter to his editor at Faber & Faber, G wrote: 'If you want to publish the book, you might suggest to the designer of the dust-jacket that yellow is a very nice color – that is, there is so much sunshine in the poems (more and more, the later you get in the book) that it would be rather appropriate to have sunshiney colors on the cover' (F&F, 24 May 1970). His publishers acceded to this request. G, who was suspicious of most drug-inspired poetry, often commented on the method of these poems, which are mostly very conscious of tradition – of Ovid's *Metamorphoses*, of Shakespeare and Elizabethan pastoral, and of the metamorphic and visionary elements in Ezra Pound's poetry, notably in his Canto 47, which refers to Circe and the herb moly. (For Pound's poem, see G's essay 'What the Slowworm Said', SL, pp. 53–65.) *Moly* also represented a return to traditional metre from free verse and syllabics. In his own words, G 'rationalised' his decision as follows: 'The acid trip is unstructured, it opens you up to countless possibilities, you hanker after the infinite. The only way I could give myself any control over the presentation of these experiences, and so could be true to them, was by trying to render the infinite through the finite, the unstructured through the structured. Otherwise there was the danger of

the experience's becoming so distended that it would simply
unravel like fog before the unpremeditated movement of free
verse' (OP, p. 182).

'Rites of Passage'
Composed February–November 1968.

G used to say that this poem was influenced by the Californian
rock group the Doors, and the lyrics of the group's lead singer,
Jim Morrison. No particular lyric seems to be referred to in
the poem, but a song G especially admired, 'The End', includes
these suggestive verses:

> Can you picture what will be
> So limitless and free,
> Desperately in need of some stranger's hand
> In a desperate land?
>
> Lost in a Roman wilderness of pain
> And all the children are insane
> All the children are insane,
> Waiting for the summer rain.

The song, like G's poem, goes on to allude to Oedipal desire:
'And he came to a door, and he looked inside. / "Father." "Yes,
son." "I want to kill you. / Mother, I want to fuck you."' There
can be no doubt that in 'Rites of Passage' G uses such myths
and the Freudian account of them to deal with the complexities
of his own childhood and growth to manhood. The poem is
an LSD pastoral, but there is much evidence of the tradition
of metamorphic poetry mentioned above. The transformation

of the speaker may remind us of both Ovid and Shakespeare, especially Bottom's metamorphosis in *A Midsummer Night's Dream*. Furthermore, in such lines as 'See Greytop how I shine', as the poet Robert Wells has pointed out to me, one can perhaps hear echoes of Native American songs, especially those admired and imitated by Yvor Winters (see Introduction, pp. xxvii–xxix) and his wife, the poet and novelist Janet Lewis. (See G's essay 'As If Startled Awake: The Poetry of Janet Lewis', SL, pp. 66–73.)

'Moly'
Completed April 1970.

It was originally called 'The Witch', and later, 'The Witch's Drink'. The witch in question is Circe from Homer's *Odyssey*. See the epigraph, which refers to the Circe narrative in Homer's poem.

G summarised the poem's situation as follows: 'Odysseus' seaman . . . has been turned to a pig – and realises he has always had a potential piggishness in him. He searches for the moly, in the hope that it will return his piggishness to its [proper place], subordinated by "the human title", and my thought is that he will be able to control his piggishness – something everybody contains – the better from having recognized it' (Bancroft 3:18).

Line 26, 'human title': In a notebook, G writes: 'I see the human title as both something primitive & sophisticated' (Bancroft 3:18). The phrase comes from *The Two Noble Kinsmen* (1.1.224–32) by Shakespeare and John Fletcher:

1st Queen:	Thus dost thou still make good the tongue o' th' world.
2nd Queen:	And earn'st a deity equal with Mars –
3rd Queen:	If not above him, for
	Thou being but mortal mak'st affections bend
	To godlike honors; they themselves, some say,
	Groan under such a mast'ry.
Theseus:	As we are men,
	Thus should we do; being sensually subdued
	We lose our human title.

'For Signs'

Mainly written in November 1968 but completed early in 1969.

It was originally called 'Moon Poem', and later 'The Moon & the Field'. As a 'moon poem', 'For Signs' contrasts with 'Sunlight', the last poem in *Moly*; G wrote of 'the rhythm of the book' as running from moonlight to sunlight (CW, August 1971). It was influenced by the revival of astrology in the 1960s. 'The title comes from the Bible, God setting the sun and moon in the sky "for signs, and for seasons" [Genesis 1.14] . . . The moon was in Scorpio when I was born, I am told, and I am further told that that means sexual perversion . . . Part 1 is me awake in moonlight, Part 2 is dreaming, Part 3 is an essay on the moon . . .' (TT, 25 December 1968).

G wrote: 'by a chicken bowl I simply meant a bowl from which chickens on a farm eat or drink' (CP, p. 490).

'Three'
Composed August 1967.

In the 1973 article 'Writing a Poem', G wrote:

> A few years ago I found myself preoccupied by certain
> related concepts I wanted to write about . . . They were
> a familiar enough association of ideas, it's true – trust,
> openness, acceptance, innocence – but I felt them all the
> more vividly and personally the more signally I failed to
> get them into a poem . . . Then one day I was walking on
> a hill going down to the Pacific, which it met at a narrow,
> partly-sheltered beach. I came to the beach from the bushes
> and was confronted by a naked family – father, mother and
> small son. The son rushed up to me very excited, shouting 'hi
> there, hi there' in his shrill voice, and rushed away without
> waiting for an answer. I walked off and felt very happy about
> the comeliness of the scene: it had, too, a kind of decorum
> that made my mind return to it several times in the next
> few hours. I mentioned it to some friends that evening and
> to others the next day, and the day after that I realized that
> I wanted to write a poem about the naked family. I didn't
> know any more than that I wanted to preserve them on
> paper in the best way I knew, as a kind of supersnapshot,
> getting my feeling about them into my description of them. It
> wasn't till the poem was finished that I realized I had among
> other things found an embodiment for my haunting cluster
> of concepts, though I hadn't known it at the time.
>
> (OP, pp. 151–52)

'From the Wave'
Composed early 1967, completed April.

The title recalls 'On the Move' (pp. 15–16), which it 'in some way' answers (JH, p. 47). The shift from bikers to surfers is significant. 'The poem was about a rather chilly January walk along a dull beach in San Francisco with some friends. We were suddenly astonished by the appearance of a bunch of surfers. A few days later, and I was in England on a visit ... so most of it was written by my aunts' stove in [Snodland, Kent,] England' (Letter to Michael Vince, 25 January 2000).

'Street Song'
Completed May 1969.

The first draft is entitled 'Dealer's Song'. It is followed in G's notebook by the mysterious sentence 'Alyosha is a dealer' – presumably a reference to Dostoevsky's saintly hero Alyosha Karamazov (Bancroft 3:10). Alyosha is also rather mysteriously present in the late poem 'A Wood near Athens' (pp. 190–92).

This is the spiel of a dope pedlar: 'not a poem taking sides. It is no more an encouragement to take drugs than [Robert Browning's] "Porphyria's Lover" is an encouragement to murder' (G, quoted in *Worlds: Seven Modern Poets*, ed. Geoffrey Summerfield, Harmondsworth: Penguin, 1974, p. 266). The poem is modelled on Elizabethan pedlars' songs as adapted for sophisticated purposes by John Dowland in 'Fine knacks for ladies' and Thomas Campion in 'Cherry Ripe', and imitated by Shakespeare in Autolycus's songs from *The Winter's Tale*. Dowland's song, with its beautiful central line 'It is a precious jewel to be plain', was praised by Yvor Winters, notably in 'The Audible Reading of Poetry' from his book *The Function of Criticism*. This essay was of major importance to G, both in his use of metre and in his public readings.

Line 1, 'I am too young to grow a beard': recalls Hermes with 'the down just showing on his face', in the epigraph to *Moly* from Homer's *Odyssey*.

Line 6, '*Keys lids acid and speed*': drug slang – 'keys' and 'lids' are measures of marijuana, 'acid' is LSD and 'speed' is amphetamine.

Line 10, 'Acapulco Gold': In a letter to a friend, G writes: 'I have a lot of the best ever grass – it is known as Acapulco Gold and is $15 a lid, it is that good' (TT, ?30 May 1968).

Line 21, 'Pure acid – it will scrape your brain': 'I won't turn into an angel and I won't go mad, but it does burn the chromosomes very nicely and doing so cleans a nice hole in the brain which can be filled by what one chooses to put there' (TT, undated letter, prob. 13 January 1969).

'Grasses'
Composed during 1969, completed September of that year.

Originally titled 'Kirby's Cove', then 'The Fort at Kirby's Cove'. G called it 'my first French Symbolist poem' (TT, 13 February 1970).

'The Discovery of the Pacific'
Composed autumn 1968 to mid-1969.

Originally called 'The Opening of the West'. The published title recalls that of a rejected poem of this period called 'The Discovery of San Francisco'. It was about adolescent lovers and was presumably meant to be paired with this one.

'[T]hese two are part of the . . . wave of 1967-ers crossing America for the Summer of Love in San Francisco' (TT, undated, ?1969).

'Sunlight'
Composed April 1967.

'[M]y favourite poem by myself' (F&F, 24 August 1992). Soon after writing the poem, G said: 'I'm very aware . . . of the division between that part of a man that seeks to define – defining is a process of choice, so of limitation, so of rejection – and that part of him that seeks to accept the world. I do not think that they should exclude each other – if they do, the man is impoverished – and both parts are always there in any one man. But certainly it is likely that one will dominate over the other. In the past, I've written a lot about the defining impulse – to the point of tedium, I expect. In this next poem, which is about the sun, I realised after I had written it that I had been trying to make amends. Here I am examining the idea of acceptance. Behind it, in particular, is my memory of a huge gathering in Golden Gate Park [in San Francisco], at the end of which [Allen] Ginsberg and [Gary] Snyder and a crowd of twenty thousand people chanted to the setting sun. This is my own address to the sun' (BBC, 19 December 1968).

G, who thought of himself as neither religious nor spiritual, accepted that 'Sunlight' could be described as a hymn: '. . . the sun is like a god. At the same time I do say in the poem that it has flaws and it's all going to burn out one day . . . It's finite . . . but, to take a line of Stevens's from "Sunday Morning": "Not as a god, but as a god might be"' (PR, p. 167).

Jack Straw's Castle

Published by Faber & Faber in 1976. This highly varied collection was designed to contrast with *Moly*. 'Much of *Moly* was about dreams; this was about nightmares . . . the drug dreams of *Moly* have all gone sour in *Jack Straw* . . .' (PR, p. 176). '[T]here's a lot of uneasiness in the book . . . there's a great line from a song by [the psychedelic rock group] The Grateful Dead – "Having a hard time living the good life" – and that could be an epigraph to *Jack Straw's Castle*' (JH, p. 52). Where *Moly* evokes a peaceable kingdom visited by angels, the sequence 'Jack Straw's Castle' is dominated by the Furies.

The poems in the book's first section are quite close to the world of *Moly,* with its utopian vision of America, but already with 'Iron Landscapes' there is a political threat to the 'dream of righteous permanence, from the past'. Like the *Moly* poems, these are strictly metrical in form. The nightmarish poems in the second section are in experimental free verse, very loose in structure and, in the present editor's judgement, not very convincing. Among G's least successful works, none of them is included in this selection. I have sought to represent that side of the book with the title sequence alone. The third and final section of JSC consists mainly of autobiographical pieces, often with English settings and characters. G originally thought of calling these pieces 'English poems'. He was thinking of writing a prose autobiography at the time and succeeded in writing three essays in autobiography: 'My Suburban Muse', 'Cambridge in the Fifties' and 'My Life up to Now', all included in OP.

JSC is also the book in which G comes out as gay.

'Diagrams'
*Composed April 1970, while he was completing the Moly
poems. Earlier titles include 'Manhattan' and 'Sky Men'.*

A number of photographs exist which show men of the
Mohawk nation working high up on the Empire State Building
in New York at the time of its construction.

'Iron Landscapes'
*Composed May–June 1973. Originally titled 'American iron/
Iron Architecture', then later 'Metal Landscape/American iron
(and French Copper)'.*

'Iron Landscapes' was written during the Watergate scandal
that brought about the fall of President Richard Nixon in
1974. The United States, still entangled in the last stages of the
Vietnam War, was troubled by recurrent anti-war and anti-
government protests.

'LACKAWANNA' is indeed the name on the ferry building.
Its importance to this poem about the polity and people of
the United States, though, is in its evidently Native American
origins. The aboriginal inhabitants of North America shadow
this collection and feature prominently in the previous poem,
'Diagrams'.

'Last Days at Teddington'
Composed 1971.

On a recent visit to Britain, G had stayed with his brother, Ander,
at his home in Teddington, near Richmond upon Thames. Ander

and his family were on the point of moving house.

'Jack Straw's Castle'
Begun in about September 1973, completed 1974.

'Night Work' seems to have been an alternative title at one stage, but the present title was an option from the beginning.

From late 1972 onwards there are occasional references in G's notebooks to gorgons and ghouls, the dark side of drug culture, nightmare and the (Charles) Manson family (see p. xxxvii). He had also been reading Dante, in particular the *Inferno*, and at one point he notes: 'I'd like to write a poem that was about leather, cocaine, gardening, Dante, the Grateful Dead, cats, and Caravaggio' (1973, Bancroft 3:32): all long-standing obsessions and enthusiasms of G's, most of which are gathered into 'Jack Straw's Castle'. In another note about 'the central section', G says: 'It is a poem about sickness, so this must be the central sickness – the central self-destructiveness, oneself stoking the fires that burn the self in a central courtyard' (Bancroft 3:34, notebook XIV). The same notebook includes this remarkable note:

> the (sudden) unavoidable realization of how self-destructive I am . . . when I have always – <u>always</u> – assumed I was the opposite. Maybe needs thinking out in terms of dreams, also in relation to my confusion of values.
>
> How <u>do</u> I work out the relation of my in general hippie values, I mean I do believe in love & trust etc, & then the other thing? I say that s & m [sadomasochism] is a form of love. I think it is, but I don't think that goes quite deep enough.

In notebook XV (Bancroft 34:36, begun 10 July 1974), G notes an answer to George Orwell's question 'does one "accept" the concentration camps?': 'one accepts them in the sense not of approving them but in the sense of acknowledging that one is part of them – they are a room in my castle.' He adds: 'also the idea of being loose in one's own castle'.

The first drafts of sections 1 and 2 of the published text are preceded by a note dated 13 September:

Idea for an open series:

Freaks/Spectral Mutations/Spectral Faeces

i.e. freaks of the imagination, but also a glance at the sense of 'deformed people', and more than a glance at the sense of heads as freaks

So: grotesques, or irrational images rising from trips and dreams. Night-work (isn't that Freud's phrase?).

G also wrote: 'the Oxford Dictionary defines Jack Straw as "a 'straw man'; a man of no substance, worth, or consideration". A pub in Hampstead is called Jack Straw's Castle, but I just took the name and intended no allusions to Hampstead in the poem' (CP, p. 491). In an interview, G also mentioned that 'one of many songs that I like from the Grateful Dead [is] called "Jack Straw"' (PR p. 176). At a poetry reading G gave when he was still working on the poem, he remarked that the castle stands for the body: the building in which one's consciousness resides. While he was writing it, he was moving house: 'I had a series of anxiety dreams. I had moved into the wrong house. I had moved in with the wrong people. Once to my horror I found I was sharing an apartment with [President] Nixon. Very often I would keep discovering new rooms in the house that I'd known nothing about' (WS, p. 11).

The poem includes many literary references, though not ones which need to be picked up: 'I was reading Dante at the time, so lots of references to the *Inferno* come in . . . The kittens changing into the Furies came from *Through the Looking-Glass*, when the kittens change into the Red Queen and the White Queen and so on. There's a bit from *Kidnapped* when David Balfour's walking up some stairs and suddenly there's a great gap' (PR, p. 176). Another influence from childhood reading is probably Beatrix Potter's uncharacteristically disturbing story *The Tale of Samuel Whiskers, or The Roly-poly Pudding*. As a small boy, G identified with the mischievous hero of that story, Tom Kitten, who, exploring the chimney of a house, loses himself in its dark recesses and is then kidnapped by rats.

Section 1, lines 1–3: probably an allusion to Baudelaire's 'L'Ennui': 'Je suis comme le roi d'un pays pluvieux' (I am like the king of a rainy country). Section 9, line 10 also seems indebted to this poem.

Section 2: 'a transcription of something I heard through my bathroom window' (JH, p. 52).

Section 8, line 15: 'inventions of Little Ease': In his introduction to *Selected Poems* of Fulke Greville (London: Faber & Faber, 1968), G quotes a passage from Greville's *Caelica* CII, in which 'strange witchcrafts, which like pleasure be / . . . do at open doors let frail powers in / To that strait building, Little-ease of sin.' G comments as follows on this passage:

[A]s part of fallen Nature, we contain our own confusions.

The possibility of a hell in the human mind anticipating the Hell after death is a constant theme of Greville's. Another theme, an almost universal preoccupation of medieval and Elizabethan writers, is that of the mutability of all Nature . . . If you put your trust in the temporal and the finite, you are putting your trust in what will inevitably fail you.

The last observation was not new, nor was it confined to Elizabethans. Similarly [Albert] Camus called life in a temporal world without sanction 'absurd' . . . Interestingly enough, Camus also used the image of Little-ease (*le malconfort*), the cell where one cannot stand, sit, or lie, for the state of a man constrained by a sense of guilt in a world where there is no god and thus where there can be no redemption for that guilt . . . Camus's great contribution is less the analysis of the sickness into which we are born than in the determination to live with that sickness, fully acknowledging it and accepting it as the basis for our actions.

(OP, p. 67)

Section 11, last line: 'Jack's ready for the world.' '[T]he point is that Jack is speaking about himself in the third person, and when do people do that? – when they're not very sure of themselves. Richard III says "Richard's himself again" [a line included in Shakespeare's play by the eighteenth-century actor-manager Colley Cibber]. There's a certain bravado in that last section, since he's uttering conditional clauses: there's no certainty he won't have to make the nightmare journey again' (JH, pp. 51–52).

'An Amorous Debate'

Begun spring 1971. 'Leather Kid and Fleshly' was originally the title.

The amorous debate is a subgenre of Elizabethan poetry. Such poems purport to be philosophical discourses in which the speaker attempts to persuade a young woman to abandon her virginity. Examples include John Donne's 'The Extasie' and Andrew Marvell's 'To His Coy Mistress'. G's poem is a playful tribute to such poems, which often involve a touch of self-parody. In Shakespeare's poem *Venus and Adonis*, where the goddess plays the male seducer's role, she reclines on a 'primrose bank' and urges Adonis to 'Bid me discourse'. She does so 'gleamingly': 'Love is a spirit all compact of fire, / Not gross to sink, but light, and will aspire' (lines 145, 149–50).

The ending of G's poem appears to allude to the French Renaissance poet Maurice Scève (?1501–*c*.1563). This seems probable, though when I mentioned it to G, he did not remember having read Scève. This is the passage in question:

N'apperçoy tu de l'Occident le Rhosne
Se destourner et vers Midy courir,
Pour seulement se conjoindre à sa Saone
Jusqu'à leur Mer, ou tous deux vont mourir?

('Have you not noticed how the Rhône changes its westward course to run towards the south, just to unite with its [tributary the] Saône and flow to the sea together, where both of them will die?')

'Autobiography'

Composed August 1972. An alternative title for the first draft was 'If I Wrote my Life'.

In the early 1970s G began working on an autobiography and, in a notebook of 1972, he wrote the opening pages, set out his plan for it and wrote a few reflections, such as the following: 'I want to get the feel of a single, complicated, interesting experience, keeping nothing back at all (for the completeness, not for the egotism) . . . behind the events, then : (1) interpretation of the events (2) reproduction of the "atmosphere", i.e. the sniff of the air (3) the public events of the time (4) the seeming digressions . . . that shd add to the inclusiveness of the moving picture dominated by the consciousness whose activity is continually aiming at further inclusion' (1972, Bancroft). The idea was eventually abandoned, but some of the material went into three essays – 'My Suburban Muse' (1974), 'Cambridge in the Fifties' (1977) and 'My Life up to Now' (1979), all reprinted in OP – and some, such as the above quotation, into poems in the third part of JSC.

'Yoko'

Composed 1974.

G wrote: '"Yoko" was a Newfoundland dog. The poem takes place on July 4, in New York, hence the fireworks' (CP, p. 491). 'I wanted to write a poem that is completely doggy, since so many poems about animals – by [D. H.] Lawrence, Marianne Moore, or Ted Hughes – are marvellous, but the subjects are dealt with from a human point of view' (JH, p. 53). Yoko's owner was Allan Noseworthy, the friend mourned in 'Lament' (pp. 167–71).

The uncharacteristic versification of this poem is indebted mainly to Lawrence and Lawrence's master, Walt Whitman. 'It seems to me that a good deal of D. H. Lawrence's free verse is very close to prose. I like it for that. Some is more incantatory, some is more biblical, but some of it is not' (PR, p. 164).

Line 32, 'I can place it finely': 'I was delighted that I could even find a Jamesian phrase at one point when the dog is sniffing a turd' (JH, pp. 53–54).

The Passages of Joy

Published by Faber & Faber in 1982. G described it as a book full of other people. 'I like the idea of a populated book. I've always liked the idea of a book of poems as a kind of . . . if not a world, a country in a world' (PR, p. 183). It is also a book about friendship: 'That was quite self-conscious . . . [Friendship] must be the greatest value in my life . . . I write about love, I write about friendship. Unlike Proust, I think that love and friendship are part of the same spectrum. Proust says that they are absolutely incompatible. I find that they are absolutely intertwined' (PR, pp. 184–85).

The title – also the epigraph to the sequence 'Transients and Residents' – comes from Samuel Johnson's melancholy satire 'The Vanity of Human Wishes'. G intended 'passages' as a pun. As Johnson uses it, it means periods of passing time. For G they are also physical passages, in particular the orifices of the body as the sources of physical pleasure. The following quotation from a notebook of G's from this period also bears on the title:

> for a Mine Shaft [examination?]
>   I have images of transition
>   anterooms
>   ladders
>   staircases
>   passage ways
>   trapdoors
>
> These are all places in between (images of foreplay)

PJ is also very much a book about middle age, about time

passing and joys still living, though soon to pass. Most of the friends are old friends, witnesses to change and decay. 'Transients and Residents', a poem about old friends, and as often critical as affectionate, is balanced by 'Talbot Road', G's tribute to his most valued friend, Tony White, who died prematurely in his forties.

PJ is in three parts. The poems about friends, much the weightiest in the book, occupy its third part. The first consists of anecdotal poems, mostly 'to do with ordinary life', all of them in free verse. Not many of these are included in the present selection. A plan for the poems in the second part is set down in the notebook just quoted from (Bancroft 3:39, 29 May 1989–May 1990). Their style, G says, is to be 'song-like, tending to the accentual, song-like but a touch gnomic, limited in a certain sense (in that they are not ample and reasonable like the verse of [Wallace Stevens's] Sunday Morning), but capable of leaps and jumps and good mysteries. I should like the content . . . to deal with night life and the compulsive and allusive life of the senses (as opposed to the level and everyday life of the poems in Part One). The surface is always interesting, because we live there so much, but it is also interesting just beneath the surface – still conscious but rather wilful and not very moral or "healthy" always.'

'Expression'
Begun May 1977 as two lines: 'The massive indifference of the altarpiece to Self, / They are expressionless.'

Writing in praise of Yvor Winters, G remarks: 'It would have seemed to him an insult to the poem that it could be used as a gymnasium for the ego' (OP, p. 176).

'Sweet Things'
Composed mid-1978. Initially called 'On my Street'.

One of G's many poems about 'the life of the street'.

'June'
Composed 1980.

About G's relationship with Mike Kitay.

'San Francisco Streets'
Begun 1979.

G loved Elizabethan song and in several poems throughout his
life drew on its manner and conventions. This is a fine example.
(Cf. 'Tamer and Hawk', p. 9, and 'Street Song', pp. 94–95.)
He was also keen on the lyrics of contemporary pop songs
and wrote a short article about those of the Beatles and their
contemporaries ('The New Music', *The Listener*, 78 (2001),
3 August 1967, pp. 129–30).

'Transients and Residents'
Begun about June 1979 and completed (or interrupted) 1980.
'Crystal' came first, then 'Falstaff' soon afterwards. 'Crosswords'
was started early in 1980, and 'Interruption' (originally called
'Delayed Preface') in the middle of the year.

For the epigraph, see headnote to this collection, p. 249 above.
   In a letter to his Faber editor, G writes: 'I envisaged this

[sequence] as being rather ambitious, maybe as many as twenty poems, each one dealing with somebody I know' (SL, p. 222). In the event there were only four, the first three about old friends – Jere Fransway ('Falstaff'), Chuck Arnett ('Crystal') and Don Doody ('Crosswords') – and the fourth about G himself.

'The first four poems are about distance, tho w[ith] DD [i.e. Don Doody] the distance is not from me, it is from an earlier part of his life. . . . Interruption . . . is part of the procedure of the series. (Interruption is the subject as well as the form of the poem.)' (Bancroft, 1978–79).

'Talbot Road'
The first draft of this poem seems to have been written quite fast, all five parts of it, towards the end of 1979. It was then taken up again in the summer of 1980 and revised.

G spent the academic year 1964–65 in Britain. He rented a flat in Talbot Road in the Notting Hill district of London, not far away from his friend, the former actor Tony White, who was then working as a translator from French and writing a guide to London pubs. White died as a result of a footballing accident in 1974 at the age of forty-five. While he was in London, G completed 'Misanthropos', which he perhaps refers to when he says at the end of section 1, 'I too tried / to render obscure passages into clear English', the passages there also alluding to the title of this collection. Discussing the hidden lives of gay people and the relief of coming out, G referred to a metaphor in this poem 'where I speak about the canals which are there all over London, but you never know they're there unless you happen to be on top of a bus: they're hidden behind walls and fences mostly' (PR, p. 177).

Of the form, G writes: 'I am trying to use the old English 4-stress line as a kind of base, which can be moved away from into a barely related free verse, but is always returned to, so is meant to be hovering in the background. I suppose I get this idea from Pound's second Canto and Basil Bunting's Briggflatts . . .' (JH/Bancroft, 1980).

Of the styles, he writes: 'I wonder if I wasn't <u>trying</u> for something less memorable in the sense of taking away striking phrases like a squirrel taking a pretty stone to gloat over in its nest. I think I was aiming at something, a discourse perhaps, of a less dense and so less priable-apart texture' (ibid.).

Section 2, line 12: 'the rich are different from us' – an allusion to the beginning of F. Scott Fitzgerald's story 'The Rich Boy' in *All the Sad Young Men* (1926): 'Let me tell you about the very rich. They are different from you and me. They possess and enjoy early, and it does something to them, makes them soft where we are hard, and cynical where we are trustful, in a way that, unless you were born rich, it is very difficult to understand.' G greatly admired Fitzgerald's prose.

Section 2, line 17: Lucio in *Measure for Measure* says: 'By my troth, Isabel, I lov'd thy brother. If the old fantastical Duke of dark corners had been at home, he had lived' (4.3.151–53).

Section 5, line 18, 'the just and the unjust': cf. 'your Father which is in heaven . . . maketh his sun to rise on the evil and on the good, and sendeth rain on the just and on the unjust' (Matthew 5.45).

'Night Taxi'
Begun mid-1980, finished by October 1981.

Dedication: Rod Taylor was a creative writing student of G's who published one exciting collection of poems, *Florida East-Coast Champion* (San Francisco, CA; Straight Arrow Books, 1972), then disappeared from San Francisco, leaving behind both literary friends and the world of poetry publishing. His disappearance was of a piece with the mobile Californian lifestyle his poetry exemplifies, and which G, from SM onwards, admired. The insistent Whitmanesque 'I' of G's poem and its versification owe something to Taylor's work.

Line 1: 'Open city'. On first arriving in California in 1954, G fell in love with the city that was to be his home: 'I went several times into San Francisco. It was still something of an open city, with whore-houses flourishing for anybody to see. A straight couple took me to my first gay bar, the Black Cat. It excited me so much that the next night I returned there on my own. And I remember walking along Columbus Avenue on another day, thinking that the ultimate happiness would be for Mike and me to settle in this city. It was foggy and I remember exactly where I thought this, right by a cobbler's that still stands there' (OP, p. 176).

The place names in this poem are all in San Francisco. 'It thrilled me to write a litany of names in "Night Taxi" . . . There are two lines where I take four extreme points in the city: "China Basin to Twin Peaks, / Harrison Street to the Ocean." I loved doing that. It's pure litany; it's not meaningful. But it gave me a feeling of possession or achievement – to have found a place for those names' (PR, p. 184).

G wrote: 'the driver must be glad, at the end of the poem, that rain will bring him more business' (CP, p. 491), and 'Did you spot my little theft from Keats at the very end . . . He has some bleak elm-tops somewhere in his unrhymed sonnet called I think . . . What the Thrush Said' (CW, 19 October 1981). Keats's line is 'And the black elm tops 'mong the freezing stars'.

The Man with Night Sweats

Published by Faber & Faber in 1992. The impact of this
collection was greater than that of any of G's later books. The
last section of it represents his response to the AIDS epidemic,
which in the mid-1980s hit San Francisco in particular.
In the course of it G lost many friends and innumerable
acquaintances. He describes the experience of living through
this plague in a letter to the poet Belle Randall, dated 9
October 1987. (Charlie is the poet Charlie Hinkle, with whom
G was in love.)

> I was touched by your letter, which was loving and
> reassuring. No, I don't have AIDS, and appear to be in
> splendid health, as does every surviving member of the house.
> I say surviving, because we did lose Jim . . . he lived upstairs
> but ate with the rest of [G's household of gay men], for about
> ten years, but died last Christmas Day. It was a horrible
> illness and a painful death (at home), but I am beginning
> to realize that death (not just from AIDS) is almost always
> painful and difficult, and that the image that us sheltered
> children have always had of dying sweetly in one's sleep is
> one most seldom realized in experience. I have had other
> friends die at other times, but the worst was from August
> 8 to September 9, during which time I lost four friends –
> friends and acquaintances – two of them on the same day.
> After the first three I thought I was holding up surprisingly
> well, but the fourth one – poor Charlie who was only thirty,
> and so full of promise – really did me in. So I have been
> having a rather hard time, which I tell you about not so you
> should feel sorry for me but so you may know what has been

happening to me and also the reason for my silence!

. . . I'll throw in some poetry with this letter. I sure have been writing a lot of it this last year. <u>Death</u> has a way of concentrating the imagination, certainly.

(BR/Bancroft 1:3, 15 January 1984–9 October 1987)

In an important introductory essay to a US reissue of MNS (New York: Farrar, Straus & Giroux, 2007), the poet August Kleinzahler associates the voice of G's mature poetry with the influence of Elizabethan poetry, particularly that of Ben Jonson. In Jonson's work, he argues, 'there's no identifiable personality to the "I", the voice in the poetry. Even in the most intimate of poems, the voice is detached, impersonal.' He goes on to describe G's admiration for those poems of Jonson's that are written in 'the plain style': 'clear in diction and movement, devoid of rhetoric and poetic figures, inclining toward the way people speak without sounding colloquial'. Kleinzahler then quotes G's essay on Ben Jonson, in which G defends Jonson against the charge that his poetry is merely 'occasional': 'All poetry is occasional, whether the occasion is an external event like a birthday or a declaration of war, whether it is an occasion of the imagination, or whether it is in some sort of combination of the two' (pp. x–xi). The deaths of friends, patrons and his own children were among Jonson's most frequent occasions, and it is impossible to read G's elegies without recalling Jonson's 'On his First Sonne', 'An Elegie on the Lady Jane Pawlet', 'To the Immortall Memorie, and Friendship of that Noble Paire, Sir Lucius Cary, and Sir H. Morison' and many others: for their valuation of friendship and different forms of attachment, for their unadorned manner, for the deep poignancy of their stoical reticence.

Of friendship G says: 'It seems to me that one of my subjects is friendship, the value of friendship . . . And if you're a writer and you have a lot of friends who suddenly die, then you're going to want to write about it. And then, one of the oldest subjects is how you face the end. One thing I've been greatly struck by in the people I've watched die is the extraordinary bravery with which people face death. So many of one's values – for humanist atheists like myself, as opposed to religious people – arise in confrontation with death' (SL, p. 229). In one poem, 'The Missing', G evokes the 'Image of an unlimited embrace', of which he says: 'I mean partly friends, partly sexual partners, partly even the vaguest of acquaintances, with the sense of being in some way part of a community' (PR, p. 158). That embrace, anticipated by the volume's opening poem, 'The Hug', which is quite unconnected with the epidemic, runs all through MNS. G was 'profoundly grateful' for a review of it by Hugh Haughton in the *Times Literary Supplement* (1 May 1992), in which the critic 'traced the imagery of touching and embracing and holding hands – and even embracing oneself at one point . . . That was not planned, it was due to the consistency of my own mind. We all have that kind of consistency of course. It's a question of opening yourself up to what you really want to say, to what for you is the truth . . .' (PR, p. 156).

'The Hug'
Composed September 1980.

In Bancroft notebook, 28 September 1981 to October 1983, G writes: 'OK, Gunny, try to write 10 rimed poems in 10 weeks. Favor irreg[ular] line length (the On my P[icture] left in Scotland form), using rhyme and <u>risk</u> the faux naif for the sake of the complexities of effect to be got from that form. Aim

for brilliance, concentration, music, surprise, inclusiveness.'
'The Hug' was the first of these, but most of the others planned
came to nothing. 'On my Picture left in Scotland' is a poem by
Ben Jonson.

'It was not sex': quoted from John Donne's 'The Extasie':

This ecstasy doth unperplex
   (We said) and tell us what we love,
We see by this, it was not sex,
   We see we saw not what did move . . .
                                    (lines 29–32)

'The Differences'
*In a notebook dated 9 December 1983–21 August 1984. First
called 'An Other/Dark Ray from Mars', then later 'Others./
An Other/Other/We Are Not Each Other', and later still
'Difference/The Difference/The Differences'.*

This poem is addressed to Charlie Hinkle, a poet and graduate
student to whom G was deeply attached. He was soon
afterwards to contract AIDS (see 'The J Car', pp. 175–76.)
G agreed with the present editor that the poem resembles a
Romantic ode: 'That is *exactly* what I wanted, and I did at
one time think of numbering the stanzas, and would have, if
the penultimate stanza hadn't ended with a comma' (CW, 28
August 1984).

The notebook in which this poem is drafted includes the
following note:

Jan 22 (Sat.): I wake beside Charlie. I have slept all night in
awareness of his body. We have not slept in a hug, precisely,

but always in contact, lightly, an arm about a waist, bodies
touching at the hips, or at the farthest with our feet resting
against each other. He was there in each dream, he was there
putting the bedclothes back over my shoulder exposed to the
cold, he was there like me falling asleep again to the sound
of small rain. To wake together is a deeply shared intimacy,
preceding words. (You can wake with a cat or dog too, &
the animal waking with you will stretch and stare trustingly
into your eyes, knowing that you understand the shared
experience).

Then to awake to see that tough but pretty face lying
on the pillow in its frothing cascade of long blond hair
is to waken into a securely grasped excitement – to wake
possessed and possessing – into a further more active
content, as I grasp your enormous hardening cock[.]

Line 14, 'the boy with iron teeth': 'I . . . meant the reader
to think of a predatory monster. He actually is a character
in a science fiction novel called *Ubik*, by Philip K. Dick (a
wonderful book), but there might be overtones of the Witch
Baby in Russian fairy tales, where witches always have iron
teeth' (ibid.).

Line 37, 'the will was lost': 'This was a very conscious
reference back to my overuse of the word *will* in my early
books . . . [it is] not *willed* love at all. I'm saying in a sense
that I'm no longer the same person as I was then and I'm
pleased that I'm not the same person . . . there is a certain
consciousness of themes but, at the same time, there's a certain
blessed unconsciousness' (PR, pp. 155–56).

The italicised passage is probably the only piece of verse
translation in G's oeuvre. It is a stanza by the Italian poet
Guido Cavalcanti, for whom see note on p. 230. Cavalcanti

was edited, translated and much celebrated by Ezra Pound, especially for the poem translated here, the *canzone* 'Donna mi priegha'. This is a philosophical lyric about the ideal of profane love which lies behind Dante.

'Skateboard'

Begun soon after 28 September 1981. Previously called 'Stylist on Haight St' and 'A Stylist'.

'[S]upposed to go with "Well Dennis O'Grady" and "Outside the Diner" [neither of which has been included here] as a sort of dwarfish triptych of the streets' (CW, 5 January 1984). But 'Skateboard' also seems to be a late response to 'On the Move' (pp. 15–16) and 'From the Wave' (pp. 92–93).

'To Isherwood Dying'

Composed 1985, finished (as G tells us) in Christmas week.

The novelist Christopher Isherwood (1904–86) and his close friend W. H. Auden influenced G in his earliest writings. Both of them 'were good influences, I think. They write simply and clearly, yet there's great complexity always there' (WS, p. 9). As he matured, G grew away from Auden, but continued to be drawn to Isherwood and his transparency of style. He met Isherwood around 1955 and they quickly became friends. There was, no doubt, an element of identification. Isherwood was as openly gay as it was possible to be in his era and, since 1939, had lived in California, providing G with a model of the uprooted, West Coast, Anglo-American writer. See G's essay/memoir, 'Christopher Isherwood: Getting Things Right'

(SL, pp. 173–96). This elegiac lyric refers to the period in the early 1930s which Isherwood spent in Berlin enjoying the sexual freedoms of the Weimar Republic. G alludes to the interlinked stories collected as *Mr Norris Changes Trains* (1935) and *Goodbye to Berlin* (1939), as well as to the memoir *Christopher and His Kind* (1976).

'The Stealer'

Begun 1984–85. Originally called 'The Thief', then 'Thievery/ Cupidon/Stealing/The Stealer'.

In an interview G said: 'It was so obvious [that desire and death are linked] during those years with AIDS. I hadn't thought of them as connected before. I don't think of sex as a self-destructive impulse, but I do view it that way in one or two poems in [MNS], like "The Stealer"' (CH).

'Nasturtium'

Completed 1985. A rough draft appears in a notebook dated 28 September 1981–October 1983. It developed through a didactic meditation called 'Song of the Garden' to the final version.

This was originally to have been one of G's 'SF sketches' of the street, such as 'Skateboard' (p. 160). The first draft read as follows:

The city of time:
he bobs within the grid,

sleeps in abandoned cars.
Not young not middle-aged not old
he fumbles through his unpaved routines.
Certain agencies keep him alive
but he's part of nobody's scheme,
not even his own.

A poor weed,
unwanted scraggle tufted
with unlovely yellow,
persists between paving stones
bearded face turned toward light.
                    (Bancroft, 1981–83)

It took 'something like three years, off and on' for this early
draft to become the finished version (SL, p. 221).

'The Man with Night Sweats'
First drafted autumn 1984; returned to and finished 1985–86.
First headed 'Poem spoken by a dying man: Night Sweats'.

G considered himself lucky never to have contracted AIDS,
though he must have feared he would do so. The speaker of
this poem 'wakes sweating in the night and assumes he has
AIDS, since one of the first symptoms of AIDS may be night
sweats' ('Poet of the Month', BBC Radio 3, 5 September 1989).

'Lament'
Drafted in a notebook dated 9 December 1983–21 August 1984. Early titles included 'On A Death/Illness & Death/On an Illness', also 'The Sickness'.

Allan Noseworthy, the owner of the dog called Yoko (see pp. 123–25, note on pp. 247–48), died of AIDs in 1985. G agreed to care for him in his last weeks of life. This was the first of G's elegies for AIDS victims. In the notebook in question (Bancroft 4:5), G writes:

Now, as when T[ony] W[hite] died I lost the London I had acquired through him, so now AN3 [Allan Noseworthy III] has died I have lost the NY I have acquired thro him . . .

The way his humor was not just frivolous in effect, it was part of a total vision that made sense; the way he was fun to be with but more than fun, his goodness. Yet no one will ever make me laugh as much again . . .

After his death (June 22): sitting in the yard: it is like being rocketed through a tunnel of days – constant return to the bed in the hospital van – thro the last month & suddenly ending in the still dense heat of this yard, flowers and weeds and bushes rising around me as in a pit of heat – I have come to a grinding halt with extreme suddenness & experience a kind of jetlag.

. . . Allan was not ready to die. Tired & ill, yet the illness so recent he was still hungry for life, he did not seem to have a mind in a state of peace or acceptance of death.

The full name of what Allan died of is pneumocystis carinii pneumonia[.]

'On ne taquine pas un malade qui dort. On l'inspecte.' Cocteau . . .

In weeks or months after the death, I keep <u>catching</u> myself as I think 'Yes, that's something I must tell Allan, that wd make him laugh, or that wd interest him', suddenly to remember that this is something I can't do any more, store jokes and stories and tho[ugh]ts away for him.

Of the poem's imagery, G wrote: 'While my friend was dying I was reading [Francis] Parkman's history of *The Jesuits in North America*, which – too easily – entered the poem. At some stage, realising that the seventeenth century reference implied was a bit much in a poem which in various ways might already have been a little close to Jonson's and Donne's elegies on the dead and dying, I tried to take out the Canadian reference – but it was stuck there, subsequent images depended on it' (CW, 28 August 1984).

'Terminal'
Composed 1986.

In the acknowledgements to MNS, G notes that this poem is about Jim Lay, who had lived in what G jokingly called his 'queer household' (PR, p. 140).

Line 12, 'Oedipus, old, led by a boy': a reference to Sophocles' play *Oedipus at Colonus*. In an early version, it was 'King Lear led by a boy'.

'Her Pet'
Composed 1987.

The marble monument evoked in this poem is to the memory of Valentine Balbiani (1518–72). It is in the Louvre and was sculpted by Germain Pilon (1525/30–90). It was erected in 1583 and includes a ghastly cadaver, a sculpture of the lady's skeleton. G came across pictures of the monument in a book on Renaissance sculpture.

'The J Car'
Composed in the course of 1988.

The poem began, probably in 1987, as a lament for the four of G's friends who had died in a single month that year. The first draft is titled 'These Four' and has an epigraph from the Ghost in *Hamlet*, 'Unhouseled, disappointed, unannealed', which resurfaces in the finished version in the line 'Unready, disappointed, unachieved'. Towards the end of the notebook, however, the poem acquires its present title, on one occasion with the subtitle 'Pastoral and Idyll', which is perhaps an attempt to place it in the English tradition of elegies for poets who have died young: such poems as Milton's 'Lycidas', Shelley's 'Adonais' and Arnold's 'Thyrsis'. Later on, the subtitle becomes 'Pastoral, Idyll, Complaint'.

The title refers to a San Francisco streetcar route. Of the subject, Charlie Hinkle, G wrote: 'The approach of death to the young and healthy gives rise in me to the tritest sentiments, but it is so very sad. I keep having the image in my mind of a body being crushed by a mountain, the crushing gradual, complete, and absolutely irreversible.' Recording Hinkle's death, he wrote: 'Of all the deaths, the only time I wouldn't have minded dying too' (JH/Bancroft, 1986).

'The Missing'

Begun 1987. Early titles include 'The Deaths of Friends', 'Plague Years' and 'Self Pity'.

'Image of an unlimited embrace' (line 12) refers to the '"gay community" (a phrase I always thought was bullshit, until the thing was vanishing) . . . I mean partly friends, partly sexual partners, partly even the vaguest of acquaintances . . .' (PR, p. 158).

Line 14, 'some ideal of sport': 'If you use the idea of sport, you think of the violence of the push, yes, but there's an ambiguity: an embrace can be a wrestler's embrace or it can be an embrace of love . . . But if you look at it at any one moment, if it's frozen, it could be either, and maybe the two figures swaying in that embrace are not even quite sure which it is. Like Aufidius and Coriolanus: they embrace, they're enemies. They embrace in admiration at one point' (PR, pp. 158–59).

Boss Cupid

Published by Faber & Faber in 2000. G's final collection is, in many ways, a continuation of his previous book. When he had finished compiling MNS, there were poems left over which eventually found their way into BC. The opening poem, 'Duncan', was begun as early as 1988, when he was still involved with writing about AIDS, and it continues the preoccupation with elegy, as does the poem on his mother's death, 'The Gas-poker', from 1991.

The second section, 'Gossip', mainly represents G's playful side. All the poems are in loose free verse and almost all of them are funny. I found it almost impossible to extract representative samples without making them seem slighter than they are. In the event, I chose the two weightiest of the poems – a self-portrait and another lament for a dead friend, 'To Donald Davie in Heaven'.

Despite the range of it, BC, as the title suggests, is primarily a book about love. It is so especially in its third section, which includes two sequences: 'Troubadour', (which, despite the brilliance of its opening, I find uneven and have therefore decided not to include) and 'Dancing David'. 'Troubadour' is about the serial murderer and cannibal Jeffrey Dahmer. 'Dancing David' is based on passages in the biblical books of Samuel and Kings. It deals with King David as lover, particularly (in 'Abishag') as ageing lover. Between the two sequences come several reflections on love, the word encompassing a spectrum of emotions ranging from Dahmer's literal hunger for the flesh he desires to the vision of Beatrice among the blessed in Dante's *Paradiso*.

The Cupid who presides over these last poems may remind

us of G's lifelong passion for Elizabethan poetry. He has little
to do, however, with refined neoclassical fancies. He is, on the
contrary, *Boss* Cupid: a wilful bully, a trigger-happy Mafioso.
The volume that bears his name is perhaps the most carefully
planned of all G's books. It ends with the poet in the guise of
dancing David: an old man taking a bow, like Shakespeare
through his Prospero bidding farewell to the stage.

'Duncan'
*Composed over a long period. Notes for it appear in G's
notebooks in mid-1988.*

The influence of the American poet Robert Duncan (1919–88)
on G's work is substantial and well documented. There are
three essays by G on his work (OP, pp. 118–34; SL, pp.
129–142, 143–170). G writes of him as 'deliberately a poet
of process', who 'spoke of writing as a process in which, if
you were a good boy, things would come to you during the
writing. The most interesting things' (PR, pp. 173–74). As
he grew older, G became more interested in such 'openness',
though he remained in many of his poems – very strikingly and
significantly in this one – a poet of 'closure'.

The ferry anecdote in the opening section is from Duncan's
Heavenly City Earthly City (1947). The story of Duncan's fall
near Wheeler Hall at Berkeley (section 2) is G's 'memory of
escorting him from the last reading he gave in '86 (Feb 4, 86)'
(Bancroft, notes for readings, n.d.). The reference to H.D., the
poet Hilda Doolittle who published under those initials, is from
her book *Hermetic Definition* (1972).

This poem, written in a strict stanza form and using ancient
elegiac conventions, celebrates a poet famous for informality

and open-endedness. G commented on this in an interview:

> I didn't plan things in this way but it seems to be one of
> the things that I specialise in. Filtering some kind of subject
> matter through a form associated with its opposite. It's as
> though I'm taking street noises and turning them into a
> string quartet. I figure that, in that way, one finds out more
> about the potentiality of the string quartet also. One finds
> out more about the rough and unformed and also about
> the elegant as well. I was aware of doing this in the Duncan
> poem and that, in a sense, is part of my subject matter in the
> Duncan poem. I'm writing about open poetry. In fact, the
> poem ends with an image I get from the Venerable Bede: the
> sparrow flying through the top of the feasting hall – in one
> open end and out the other – and of course 'open-endedness'
> is also the characteristic of Duncan's own poetry. I'm using
> that as a kind of pun.
>
> (Clive Wilmer, *Poets Talking*, Manchester: Carcanet,
> 1994, p. 5)

Lines 43–44: 'whose great dread . . . soon to be enclosed.'
Duncan had told G that 'For [his friend the experimental poet
Charles] Olson, closure meant death' (Bancroft, notebook 3,
1980).

Line 45: 'the sparrow's flight' – an image in the Venerable
Bede's *An Ecclesiastical History of the English People*
(completed *c*.AD 731): 'the sparrow flying thro the feasting hall
of the warrior – in one end and out the other' is an image of
the course of life from birth to death. I remember G referring to
this passage in conversation as early as 1964.

'My Mother's Pride'

G's first notes for this poem are in a notebook of 1974. He began work on it, however, in 1990. Early titles include 'My Mother's Precepts', 'My Mother's Sayings' and 'Pride'.

G compared the organisation of this poem to that of Ezra Pound's 'Canto XIII', 'which is [G said in an interview] a slightly random collection of sayings by Confucius. I brought her sayings together in the same kind of way . . .' (JC, p. 19).

'The Gas-poker'

Composed 1991, unusually quickly by G's standards. An alternative to the present title was 'The Instrument'.

The first entry in G's diary is for 29 December 1944, when he was fifteen. It records the suicide of his mother, as follows:

> Mother died
> at 4.0 A.M, Friday,
> DECEMBER 29TH
> 1944 –

She committed suicide by holding a gas-poker to her head, and covering it all with a tartan rug we had. She was lying on the sheepskin rug, dressed in her beautiful long red dressing-gown, and pillows were under her head. Her legs were apart, one shoe half off, and her legs were white and hard and cold, and the hairs seemed out of place growing on them.

We had awoken at 9.45, and had dressed leisurely but were puzzled by a tender note against the parlour door, saying 'Don't try to get in. Ask Mrs Stoney to help you, darlings.'

Then we realized that both the parlour and kitchen door were locked. So we did go over to Mrs Stoney, who lives next door. But only her son was in, she having gone out shopping. Then Ander [G's younger brother] tried the back gate which was unlocked and we went in through the back door into the parlour. ~~but I guessed – though I hardly dared to even when I saw the note. I think Ander did too. But we did not dare mention our conjectures~~. Both gate and door were unlocked, and they had certainly been locked the evening before. Mother had done this, we supposed to make it easier for us to get in. Ander began to scream 'Mother's dead! She's killed herself,' before I could even realize that she was, and that her body stretched along the floor, with her hands up to her face under the loose rug.

There was a smell, but not a very ~~horrible~~ great one, of gas. It haunted us for the whole day afterwards. I turned the gas off and Ander took the gas poker out of her hands.

We didn't undo the blackout for we could see her ~~perfectly~~ well by the the light from the French window, open behind us.

We uncovered her face. How horrible it was! Ander said afterwards to me that the eyes were open, but I <u>thought</u> they were closed; she was white almost, like the rest of her body that we could see. 'Cover it up. I don't want to see it. [Illegible crossing-out.] It's so horrible,' Ander cried. Her hed [sic] was back, and the mouth was open, – not expressing anything, horror, sadness, happiness, – just open.

But oh! mother, from the time when I left you at eleven on Thursday night until four in the morning, what did you do?

She died quickly and peacefully, they said, but what agonies of <u>mind</u> she must have passed through during the night. I hate to think of her sadness. My poor, poor mother; I hope you slept most of the time, but however sad then, you are happy now. Never will you be sad again! Dear, dear, sweet mother. It was Joe [her second husband, from whom she was estranged] perhaps who caused your death. He had left the house (for the second time since their marriage), on the early morning of the 27th; I had heard his voice, through my sleep; at her command.

Oh mother, you could have called him back, but you knew we didn't like him! But we would rather you had 10,000 Joes in our house, rather than you had killed yourself.

How could we know how sad she was! I feel certain that it was after 11.20, when I came down to fetch my watch, and when I kissed her (I'm so glad I did!), that she decided to kill herself.

I kissed her legs. – Then called the police . . . I kissed her forehead when the policeman wasn't looking; poor lovely statue! At first we ran screaming into the front garden – stiff with frost.

Later in the morning, I came into the parlour to get something out of the bureau; the blackout on only one window was undone, the cat was nestling and purring with a pleased look and half-shut eyes, in the dressing gown's folds between her legs, in the dim light and disordered room . . .

In a radio interview broadcast in 2000, G said: 'She killed herself, and my brother and I found her body, which was not her fault because she'd barred the doors, as you'll see in the poem. Obviously this was quite a traumatic experience; it would be in anybody's life. I wasn't able to write about it till just a few years ago. Finally, I found the way to do it was really obvious; to withdraw the first-person, and to write about it in the third-person. Then it came easy, because it was no longer about myself. I don't like dramatizing myself' (JC, p. 19). G felt distaste for what M. L. Rosenthal called the Confessional school. This poem about a mother committing suicide may hint at one of several reasons why.

The image of the flute owes something to classical tradition: when Pan chases Syrinx she escapes him by turning into a reed. Instead of taking her virginity, he plucks the reed, makes a flute of it, and plays a lament upon it. This shows how the consolations of art are directly connected to the original loss.

Line 18, 'A burden, to each other': There is a pun here. A burden in music can be a drone (like a bagpipe), the bass accompaniment of a song, a refrain or a persistent theme.

'To Donald Davie in Heaven'
Composed in 1995, soon after the death of Donald Davie on 18 September.

A distinguished poet and critic, Davie (1922–95) was one of G's most valued literary friends. Radical and adventurous as a critic, he was by contrast politically conservative and, in religion, something of a Puritan. He and G differed fiercely on such matters, and this poem plays affectionately with their disagreements.

Regarding the title, cf. William Carlos Williams, 'To Ford Madox Ford in Heaven'.

Lines 10–12, 'those who sought honour . . . increase our loves': Dante, *Paradiso* 5.100–05. Seventeen years before this poem was written, G quoted this passage of Dante in a notebook (Bancroft 3:38, April–May 1978) and adds this translation of it:

As in a fish pool still & clear,
the fish draw to what comes from outside
in such a way that they think it their food
so did I see more than a thousand splendors
draw toward us, and in each was heard
Lo, one who shall increase our loves.

The reference is conflated with an allusion to W. H. Auden's
poem 'Fish in the unruffled lakes'.

'The Artist as an Old Man'
*Composed 1995 or 1996. An earlier title is 'Painter as Samson,
Painter as Lion'.*

Inspired by Lucien Freud's full-length nude self-portrait, *Painter
Working* (1993). Another self-portrait of Freud's, *Interior with
Hand Mirror* (1967), was chosen by G for the cover of BC.
Freud reciprocated G's admiration.

In the biblical Book of Judges, Samson kills a lion with his
bare hands. Returning to the spot later to find a woman of the
Philistines who has attracted him, he finds 'a swarm of bees
and honey in the carcase of the lion'. He takes the honey for
his parents and, later asked to explain himself, he replies with a
riddle: 'Out of the eater came forth meat, and out of the strong
came forth sweetness' (Judges 14:5–14).

'A Wood near Athens'
Composed 1994.

The poem is closely related to G's sequences 'Troubadour' and

'Dancing David' (see headnote, p. 267). Work for all three appears in the same notebook. 'Troubadour' is concerned with the gay serial killer and cannibal Jeffrey Dahmer, who exemplifies one of G's recurrent metaphors: that of *feeding* on an object of desire or the subject of a poem. 'A Wood near Athens' deals with a much wider conception of love, but includes Dahmer, both his name and what he represents for G.

G describes 'A Wood near Athens' as 'a TSE or EP-like collage' with connecting phrases left out 'so that the reader could make the connections' (JH/Bancroft, 2 November 1995). The initials are those of T. S. Eliot and Ezra Pound, and a manuscript draft is headed with the question 'A Canto?', referring to *The Cantos of Ezra Pound*. Where Pound would have used free verse, however, G writes in iambic metre.

A Midsummer Night's Dream, 'A wedding entertainment about love', is set in 'A wood near Athens'.

Line 6: Absalom is the son of King David, who rebelled against his father. When the King heard that Absolom had been defeated and was dead, he wept and said: 'O my son Absalom, my son, my son Absalom! would God I had died for thee, O Absalom, my son, my son!' (2 Samuel 18:33). The citation connects the poem with 'Dancing David' (pp. 193–97).

Line 37: Attila Richard Lukacs (b. 1962) is a Canadian painter of homoerotic subjects, mostly hyper-masculine nudes.

Line 42: 'They that have power to hurt' – Shakespeare's Sonnet 94.

The last stanza alludes to the ending of Dante's *Paradiso*.

'Dancing David'

Composed 1994. The first draft follows 'A Wood near Athens' in G's notebook.

'God': King David's first wife, Michal, was the daughter of his predecessor, Saul. The stories told of her in the two books of Samuel are sometimes contradictory. She seems to have loved David against the wishes of her father; she is also, in the passage G is using here, contemptuous of his apparently barbarous behaviour, dancing before the Ark of the Lord unclothed. See 2 Samuel 6:14–16, 18, 20–23:

> And David danced before the Lord with all his might; and David was girded with a linen ephod.
> So David and all the house of Israel brought up the ark of the Lord with shouting, and with the sound of the trumpet.
> And as the ark of the Lord came into the city of David, Michal Saul's daughter looked through a window, and saw king David leaping and dancing before the Lord; and she despised him in her heart . . .
> And as soon as David had made an end of offering burnt offerings and peace offerings, he blessed the people in the name of the Lord of hosts.
> Then David returned to bless his household. And Michal the daughter of Saul came out to meet David, and said, How glorious was the king of Israel to day, who uncovered himself to day in the eyes of the handmaids of his servants, as one of the vain fellows shamelessly uncovereth himself!
> And David said unto Michal, It was before the Lord, which chose me before thy father, and before all his house, to appoint me ruler over the people of the Lord, over Israel: therefore will I play before the Lord.

And I will yet be more vile than thus, and will be base in mine own sight: and of the maidservants which thou hast spoken of, of them shall I be had in honour.

Therefore Michal the daughter of Saul had no child unto the day of her death.

'Bathsheba': David's great sin is the killing of Bathsheba's husband because he, David, lusted after her. David married her and she became the mother of Solomon, the wisest of Hebrew kings. See 2 Samuel 11:1–4, 14–17, 26–27:

And it came to pass, after the year was expired, at the time when kings go forth to battle, that David sent Joab, and his servants with him, and all Israel; and they destroyed the children of Ammon, and besieged Rabbah. But David tarried still at Jerusalem.

And it came to pass in an eveningtide, that David arose from off his bed, and walked upon the roof of the king's house: and from the roof he saw a woman washing herself; and the woman was very beautiful to look upon.

And David sent and enquired after the woman. And one said, Is not this Bathsheba, the daughter of Eliam, the wife of Uriah the Hittite?

And David sent messengers, and took her; and she came in unto him, and he lay with her; for she was purified from her uncleanness: and she returned unto her house.

And the woman conceived, and sent and told David, and said, I am with child . . .

And it came to pass . . . that David wrote a letter to Joab, and sent it by the hand of Uriah.

And he wrote in the letter, saying, Set ye Uriah in the forefront of the hottest battle, and retire ye from him, that he may be smitten, and die. And it came to pass, when Joab observed the city, that he assigned Uriah unto a place where he knew that valiant men were.

And the men of the city went out, and fought with Joab: and there fell some of the people of the servants of David; and Uriah the Hittite died also . . .

And when the wife of Uriah heard that Uriah her husband was dead, she mourned for her husband.

And when the mourning was past, David sent and fetched her to his house, and she became his wife, and bare him a son. But the thing that David had done displeased the Lord.

'Abishag': See I Kings 1:1–4, 15–17:

Now king David was old and stricken in years; and they covered him with clothes, but he gat no heat.

Wherefore his servants said unto him, Let there be sought for my lord the king a young virgin: and let her stand before the king, and let her cherish him, and let her lie in thy bosom, that my lord the king may get heat.

So they sought for a fair damsel throughout all the coasts of Israel, and found a Shunammite, and brought her to the king.

And the damsel was very fair, and cherished the king, and ministered to him: but the king knew her not . . .

And Bathsheba went in unto the king into the chamber: and the king was very old; and Abishag the Shunammite ministered unto the king.

And Bathsheba bowed, and did obeisance unto the king. And the king said, What wouldest thou?

And she said unto him, My lord, thou swarest by the Lord thy God unto thine handmaid, saying, Assuredly Solomon thy son shall reign after me, and he shall sit upon my throne.

Index of Titles and First Lines

Poem titles are in italics. First lines are in roman.

[279]